Some Day My Prince Will Come

Some Day My Prince Will Come

A Guide for Women Whose Dream Has Not Yet Come True

by Serena Gray

A CITADEL PRESS BOOK
Published by Carol Publishing Group

A Citadel Press Book
Published by Carol Publishing Group
Citadel Press is a registered trademark of Carol Communications, Inc.
Editorial Offices: 600 Madison Avenue, New York, N.Y. 10022
Sales and Distribution Offices: 120 Enterprise Avenue, Secaucus, N.J. 07094
In Canada: Canadian Manda Group, P.O. Box 920, Station U, Toronto, Ontario
   M8Z 5P9
Queries regarding rights and permissions should be addressed to Carol Publishing
Group, 600 Madison Avenue, New York, N.Y. 10022

Carol Publishing Group books are available at special discounts for bulk
purchases, sales promotions, fund-raising, or educational purposes.
Special editions can be created to specifications. For details, contact Special
Sales Department, Carol Publishing Group, 120 Enterprise Avenue, Secaucus,
N.J. 07094

Interior illustrations by Amy Cyphers.

Manufactured in the United States of America
10 9 8 7 6 5 4 3 2 1

Library of Congress Cataloging-in-Publication Data

Gray, Serena.
     Some day my prince will come : a guide for women whose dream has not yet
come true / by Serena Gray.
       p.   cm.
     ISBN 0-8065-1510-4
     1. Man-woman relationships.   2. Interpersonal relations.   3. Mate
selection.   4. Self-help techniques.   I. Title.
HQ801.G68   1994
646.7'7—dc20   93-45557
                                                          CIP

For the researchers in New York,
Elise, Marilyn, and Françoise.

Some Day My Prince Will Come

Introduction

Some Day My Prince Will Come . . . But He Might Be Late

When it comes to relationships, everyone on this boat is a bozo.
—Susan F. Young, Eminent Psychologist

The door to my office opens. An attractive, intelligent-looking woman stands there, grasping the frame. She hesitates in the entranceway. "Dr. Gray?" she asks. Her voice quivers with hope. "Are you Dr. Serena Gray, the famous relationship crisis counselor?"

I smile, soothingly. "Good afternoon, Ms. A," I say. "Won't you please sit down?"

Ms. A nods. Slowly, like a woman in shock, she crosses the room and sits down. There is something about her that suggests to my professional eye that this woman has been sitting in a dark room eating bags of potato chips and boxes of cookies while listening to sad songs on the CD player. And indeed, up close, one can't help but notice that her skin is pale, there are crumbs caught in the folds of her blouse and dark circles around her eyes, and she is humming "Hello, Walls" very softly under her breath. Nervously clutched in one hand is a box of man-size tissues.

I lean forward slightly. I give her a warm smile. "So," I say in my most comforting voice. "How can I help you, Ms. A?"

Ms. A smiles, wanly. "Well," she says, "It's. . . . He. . . . We. . . ." She snuffles and pulls a tissue from the box. "I don't know where to start. . . ."

I smile, encouragingly. "Start at the beginning," I say. "It's always the best place."

"Of course," says Ms. A. "At the beginning." She takes a deep breath. "Yes, at the beginning." She smiles, bravely. She starts shredding the tissue in her hand. "Well, let's see. . . . I met Richard three years ago. . . . At a sponsored walk. I twisted my ankle and he . . ." She snuffles, then makes a superhuman effort to continue. ". . . Anyway, he—Richard—was the most wonderful man I'd ever known. Kind . . . sensitive . . . generous . . . funny . . . attractive . . . self-reliant . . . he could cook hot food and work a washing machine. . . . He was everything I'd ever dreamed of in a man. . . ." She yanks another tissue from the box.

"Go on," I urge, gently. "Then what happened, Ms. A?"

She smiles, ruefully. "We fell in love. . . ."

I lean back in my chair. "Yes . . . ?"

She blows her nose. "We moved in together. . . ."

I fold my hands. "And . . . ?"

"It was bliss. . . ." She jerks another tissue free.

My voice is soft. "And then?"

She bites her lip. "We were going to get married. . . ."

I nod, sympathetically.

Ms. A stares back at me in silence, a wad of tissues balled up in her hand and something rather catastrophic happening to her eye makeup.

2

Because she seems to have lost the thread, I bring us up to date on the story so far. "You twisted your ankle," I remind her. "He was perfect. You fell in love. You moved in together. It was bliss. You were going to get married. . . ."

"I can't believe it. . . ." Ms. A half wails, half whispers. "I just can't believe it . . . Richard . . . the man I loved and trusted and admired. . . . The man whose children I wanted to bear. . . . The man I let see me with henna in my hair. . . . I just can't believe it. . . . It's so incredible. . . ." Ms. A bursts into tears.

Several hours, boxes of tissues, and cups of strong coffee later, Ms. A, exhausted, slumps back in her seat, her tale all told. All the while she had been building her life around Richard Freestone, Richard Freestone had an estranged wife, two children, three guinea pigs, and a rottweiler in Jersey City. He'd meant to tell her, but somehow he never got around to it till the day before the wedding. He might not have told her then, but his estranged wife had finally begged him to come home—a request he had agreed to, because, when he thought about it, he'd never really stopping loving his estranged wife, and there were the children and the house to consider.

And Ms. A never suspected a thing?

Nope. Not a thing.

She believed what he told her. That the pictures of the gap-toothed children in his wallet were of his niece and nephew. That he was working every other weekend. That the dog hairs on his clothes belonged to the German shepherd on the first floor. She didn't think it odd that she was never introduced to his family, or that he had never invited her to his apartment, or that she never met any of his friends.

"How could I?" she sobs. "How could I have fooled myself like that?"

I bring all of my powers of understatement to the fore. "It happens," I say.

"But not to me!" wails Ms. A. "Me! I'm a president of one of the most influential advertising agencies in the world. I fly my own plane. I have a doctorate in psychology. I watch Oprah! How could I be so stupid? How could I fall for such a complete jerk?"

"Believe me," I say, "this is pretty common."

Having run out of anything else to use, Ms. A wipes her eyes on her sleeve. She stares at me. "It is?"

"You're not the first woman in the history of the world to ask herself those questions," I reassure her. "How could he? Why did he? How could I? Why didn't I? Why do I always end up sleeping with dorks?"

She knocks back the last mouthful of cold coffee. "I'm not?"

"No, you're not." I shake my head. "And I rather doubt that you'll be the last," I add.

To say that there is nothing new or unusual about Ms. A's story is to be rather sparing with the truth. Women have been wailing, "I can't believe it. . . . I just can't believe it" and bursting into tears over men since Adam bit into the apple and immediately blamed Eve for the downfall of mankind.

Indeed, from a certain perspective—the perspective of the professional relationship crisis counselor—there isn't even anything particularly interesting in Ms. A's story. Ms. A had met the man she thought was the prince of her dreams. She invested considerable time, trouble, emotion, energy, and money in him. She changed her brand of toothpaste, started wearing skirts, took up tennis, abandoned her hang-gliding class to stay home and watch television with him, learned to make fudge brownies just the way his mother made them, started naming their children and thinking more kindly about the Republicans—and what for? To discover that he wasn't the prince of her dreams after all—he was the frog of her nightmares.

So what else is new?

Let's face it, men drive women crazy. They're unreliable, undependable, bossy, opinionated, stubborn, self-centered, and selfish. They have large but fragile egos, which makes it almost impossible to travel with them over long distances or difficult

4

terrain. They have penises, which in most cases is rather like having a license to kill. They can never remember your birthday, your dress size, the names of their children, or where the corkscrew is kept. They tell you one thing and then do something else.

Not only that, but no matter how well you think you know a man—even if you've been exchanging saliva with him and washing his underpants for the last forty years—you can never really tell what's going on in that small but complex mind.

One morning you'll be getting ready to go to church, just like you have every Sunday for the last forty years, and he'll look up from the paper and say, "Oh, by the way, Angela, I won't be here when you get back."

You continue to adjust your hat in the mirror. "Playing golf?" you ask.

He folds the sports sections four times, the way he does, and shakes his head. "No," he says. "I'm moving into a trailer with that girl who works in the liquor store. . . ."

You think he's joking. You laugh. "Well don't be too long, dear," you say. "Remember the children are coming for lunch."

"I won't be here," he repeats. "I'm moving into a trailer with the girl who works in the liquor store. I'm going to become a potter and write poetry."

You laugh louder. "Of course you are, darling," you say. "What else would a corporate accountant who can't sleep without a humidifier do on a Sunday morning?"

"We're taking the trailer to Ottawa," he says.

Something in his voice makes you slowly turn around to look at him. "What?" you say as reality begins to drip in. "You're going to Ottawa in a trailer?"

He brushes toast crumbs onto the floor. "Yes," he says. "With the girl from the liquor store."

For the first time in forty years you don't tell him to stop brushing toast crumbs on to the floor. "With the blonde with the gap between her teeth?" you ask.

He gives you his trust-you-to-get-the-wrong-end-of-the-stick look. "Of course not," he says. "What kind of man do you think I am? With the one with the nose ring."

Shock keeps you from actually screeching. "But our home ..." you gasp. "Our friends ... our children ... our forty years. ... Why?" He shakes his head sadly. "Because you've never really understood me," he says.

Let's face it, you'd have to have spent your entire life in what's left of the Amazonian rain forest not to have some idea of what men are like. They won't commit. They will commit, but only when you don't want them to anymore. They should be committed. They don't love enough. They love too much and ill-advisedly. They give too little. They take too much. They hate women. They hate their mothers. They love themselves, their best friend, football, work, bull mastiffs, or their Fender twelve-string more than they will ever love a girl. They refuse to grow up. They think they have grown up. They're looking for mothers. They're looking for sisters. They're looking for adoration. They're looking for any warm place to put their penis.

In the decades between the first awkward teenage date and that last mature knock-down-drag-out domestic row in the fresh-produce section of the local supermarket, the average female in search of her prince embraces enough amphibians to merit an honorary zoology degree. Or, as my friend Amanda once commented, "It's a wonder my lips aren't green by now."

Professionals in the relationship field refer to the tendency of men to turn out to be less than they promised as "The Frog Factor."

Why do so many men seem so wonderful when you first meet them and then turn out to be total turkeys?

Why does it take a woman so long to figure out that the guy sleeping next to her with his foot in her back and all the blankets wrapped around him isn't Prince Charming but a small, moist amphibian with a voracious appetite and a liking for bogs?

Why, knowing what men are like, do women still hope to

find their prince no matter how many times they've been down to the pond?

The simple fact of the matter is that the man who—tearstained years later—turns out to be a jerk was always a jerk. Short of wearing a sign around his neck that said I AM A COMPLETE TURKEY WHO'S GOING TO BLOW UP YOUR HAIR DRYER DEFROSTING THE FREEZER AND THEN GO TO PERU, it couldn't have been more obvious. No one made you kiss him. No one made you wash his socks or listen to his stories of his time in Tanzania. No one made you put up with his little quirks or neurotic dependencies. No one made you overlook his faults or make excuses for him. The only person who fooled you into thinking he was Mr. Right when he was really Mr. Rititnitit was no one but yourself.

And whose fault is that? His?

It is time, therefore, that women stopped looking at men through the rose-colored glasses of romance. It is time to be honest; time to stop kidding ourselves. Time to take responsibility for our own mistakes. You've been on the dates. You've worked at the marriage. You've written the letters, seen the movies, and wept to the songs. You've sat in those kitchens, on those sofas, and in those wine bars, talking for hours on end to your female friends and relatives, pulling our your perm, breaking your nails, ruining your makeup, and sobbing over and over. Whywhywhywhywhy?

Now read the book.

Addicted to Love

We live in the age of the addict. Everyone, it seems, is addicted to something. Work ... alcohol ... shopping ... tobacco ... chemicals ... aspirins ... talking on the telephone ... chocolate chip cookies ... 500 rummy.... Each of us knows someone in AA or Weight Watchers. Someone who has had her credit card confiscated or who has to keep the potato chips in the trunk of the car. There is no shame these days in admitting that you have an unhealthy fondness for gin or can't pass a shoe store without dashing in for another pair of pumps.

Nonetheless, despite this new atmosphere of openness there is one addiction that is rarely spoken of or even mentioned. The addiction that, until fairly recently, had no name. And yet this addiction is not only debilitating and ultimately destructive, it is all-pervasive as well, affecting every aspect of a person's life.

You frown, puzzled. It's probably not tortilla chips or china dogs you reckon. "Drugs?" you venture.

Good guess, but no. Like drugs, this addiction will send you roaming empty, unlighted streets in the dead of night. Like drugs, it will have you slipping through dark, sleazy bars to talk in whispers to men wearing one silver snake earring and black leather gloves. And also like drugs, it will lose you sleep, your appetite, your good complexion, and your peace of mind. But unlike the addiction to drugs, this addiction is actually encouraged by society. Unlike drugs, the object of this addiction is totally legal and easily available.

"I give up," you say. "If it's not sleeping pills or rum raisin ice cream, what is it?"

It's the addiction to love. It makes strong women weak. It makes weak women mush. It makes sane, intelligent women—women who run companies and give good advice to all their friends—put up with behavior in a man that she would find totally unacceptable, not to say grounds for homicide, in anyone else.

"Addiction to love?" you ask. "You mean like the song?"

No, I mean like the addiction. I mean the insatiable craving for romance. The driving need to be part of a couple. The condition of being in love with the very idea of love. Let's face it, it's easier to kick heroin than to give up love.

"Oh, hold on," I hear you say. "I think you're going a little overboard there, Dr. Gray, comparing a natural yearning for romance with a hard-drug habit."

Do you? Then perhaps you have never heard the story of Margery Hoople.

You shake your head. You never have.

Margery Hoople was as ordinary as a slice of bread and as upstanding as a Methodist minister. She worked as a computer analyst, owned a garden apartment, and supported two cats and a cockatoo. Margery's lovelife began slowly and predictably. She dated a few boys in high school, had a steady boyfriend at college, and eventually married Stan, a man she met at a computer convention in Tokyo. They were divorced four years later.

"At first I guess I was too angry with Stan to want to be in love," says Margery. "And besides, I had a full and busy life. I didn't need some software salesman leaving his socks on my printer or accusing me of infecting his computer."

But then, as the wounds made by Stan Waldorf Hoople began to heal, Margery's attitude toward men began slowly but surely to change.

"The first thing I remember was that I began noticing couples," says Margery. "You know, in the street and in stores and places like that? It wasn't like I really missed Stan—good grief, I didn't even like Stan—but I'd see these couples smiling at each other over the meat freezer or arguing about what video to rent and I'd feel like I was missing something."

As time went on, Margery's feeling of "missing something" increased. "Here I was with a good job, and great friends and lots of interests, but when I watched television or read a magazine or saw a movie, I couldn't help but realize that my life was empty and meaningless because I was on my own."

Margery stopped watching the news and documentaries completely and concentrated on love stories and sitcoms. She started eating her frozen dinners by candlelight. She began to flip through the personal ads. She found herself reading *Wuthering Heights*.

"It was really weird how this kind of thing just sneaks up on you," says Margery. "One day you're borrowing your mother's old copy of *Gone with the Wind* and the next you're standing in the video store on a Friday night, unable to decide between *Romancing the Stone*, *Moonstruck*, and *When Harry Met Sally*—so you take out all three."

Things continued apace.

"One Friday night I came home from work, absolutely exhausted," Margery explains. "All I wanted to do was get through the door, kick off my shoes, put on some Guns 'n Roses, and fix myself a big bowl of chili. Stan hated Guns 'n Roses and chili. And then I get this phone call from a friend of mine inviting me to a party. I hate parties. I've always hated parties. All that happens at a party is you wind up in a corner miles away from the tortilla chips, listening to someone whose name you never quite catch explaining how bottle caps are made. But then, just as I was about to say I had a previous engagement, I heard this little voice whispering in my ear. Margery, said this little voice. Margery, what if Mr. Right is at this party? What if he's waiting for you by the cheese ball? If you don't go, you'll never meet him. I told the little voice that I wasn't looking for Mr. Right, and the little voice said, Well, you should be.

So what happened?

Margery rolls her eyes. "The Mr. Wrongs were stacked six-deep in every room. Plus the food was lousy. You either had to dip it into something else or shake the ashes off it. But I couldn't leave. That same little voice kept whispering in my ear, If you leave now, Mr. Right will arrive in ten minutes and end up talking to the woman in the Lycra dress. If you, his one true love, aren't here, the man you were destined to live happily ever after with will wind up marrying someone else and having the wrong children and the wrong life. Margery sighs. "So I had to stay, didn't I? I mean, that's a hell of a responsibility."

After that, Margery not only went to every party she was invited to—just in case Mr. Right should show up—she took out personal ads, she joined night classes, she started listening to the radio. "I'd never realized before how many love songs there are. I mean, pop, rock, easy-listening, country—it doesn't really matter what station you turn on. Except for Sousa marches and polkas, it's pretty much all I'll love you forever, or I'll love you forever even though you clobbered my heart." From there it was but a small step to lingering at bus stops in the rain. . . .

"Bus stops in the rain?" you query.

She found them mesmerizingly romantic. She'd put a Billie Holliday or a Whitney Houston tape in her Walkman and she'd stand there for hours. It had something to do with an old black-and-white movie she rented one night when someone else beat her to *Moonstruck*.

"So then what happened?" you rightly want to know.

What happened then was the equivalent of wrapping your baby in a blanket and going out into a blizzard at three in the morning to get a pack of cigarettes.

"It was at my sister's wedding," says Margery. She smiles, sadly but wisely. "It was like something snapped," she recalls now. "I saw my sister standing there, all in white and looking radiant and happy, and everybody congratulating her and telling her how excited they were for her, and even though no one in the family even liked her husband and my mother was taking bets that they wouldn't last the honeymoon, all of a sudden all I could hear was the music from a thousand popular songs and all I could think of was Cher and Nicholas Cage . . . Bogart and Bacall . . . Hepburn and Tracy . . . Clark Gable and Claudette Colbert in *It Happened One Night*. Suddenly I just knew that I'd die without love. I'd just shrivel up and die. That if I didn't find that one perfect person to complete me and give my life purpose I just might as well be dead."

"One person out of a world population of billions . . ." you muse. "Only one . . . ?"

So Margery believed. Only one.

"One minute I was standing beside the other women, waiting for Sharon to toss the bouquet over the banister," Margery continues, "and the next I'd knocked the maid of honor to the ground and wrenched the flowers from her hands. I'd ripped her dress and was just bending her headband in two when the ushers pulled me off her."

Addicted to Love: The Quiz

It isn't always as easy as you might think to spot the love addict. Love junkies don't necessarily have dilated pupils or dark circles around the eyes. Indeed, on the surface, they often appear completely sane and well-balanced. They didn't watch any of the royal weddings. They laughed when Bruce Springsteen's first marriage broke up. They walk out of the room whenever Rhonda Liversausage starts complaining about her boyfriend again. "Give it a rest, Rhonda," they say. "It's been fifteen years. Either dump the dork or shut up."

But scratch that surface and what do you find? You find a person who buys every daily paper she can get her hands on, just in case this is the day the stars say An affair of the heart is on the horizon. Taurus could figure in your life. You find a person who jumps for the bouquet at weddings. A person who reads through the personals, just in case. A person who stays indoors, eating take-out pizza and chowmein for an entire weekend because Lester Spinner said he might call. Someone who would rather go without the B vitamins than go without love. Someone who would rather have a significant other than a Nobel Prize. Are you one of these people? Are you a hopeless romantic? Are you hooked on love? Here's a simple quiz to test your sucker for love potential.

	Yes	No
1. My favorite time of year is spring.	——	——
2. I answer personal ads.	——	——
3. I take out personal ads.	——	——
4. I encourage others to take out personal ads.	——	——
5. I answer personal ads for my friends.	——	——
6. Given the choice between a single long-stemmed red rose and an electric screwdriver, I would always choose the rose.	——	——
7. I believe is Kismet.	——	——
8. I believe in Love at First Sight.	——	——
9. To quote the Ronettes: "It's in his kiss."	——	——
10. To quote U2: "I believe in love."	——	——
11. To quote *Passion's Prayer*: "When their lips met she finally understood what it was to be alive."	——	——
12. Love conquers all.	——	——
13. I think it's really romantic that King Edward gave up his throne for Mrs. Simpson. I would have done the same thing myself.	——	——

	Yes	No

14. I keep a supply of candles in the house, just in case. ⎯⎯ ⎯⎯

15. I have a bottle of sparkling white wine in the fridge because you never can tell. ⎯⎯ ⎯⎯

16. The reason I cry at weddings is that I'm so happy ⎯⎯ ⎯⎯

17. I love musical comedies. ⎯⎯ ⎯⎯

18. I just know Rhett and Scarlet got back together. ⎯⎯ ⎯⎯

19. I think the world can always use another love song. ⎯⎯ ⎯⎯

20. I often imagine myself walking along a sandy beach in the moonlight beneath the swaying palms ⎯⎯ ⎯⎯

21. In the above fantasy, it is never monsoon season, and I am never alone. ⎯⎯ ⎯⎯

22. I would never keep a pack of condoms on hand. It seems too passionless and unspontaneous ⎯⎯ ⎯⎯

23. I believe that the hero and heroine going off into the sunset/the 7-Eleven/deepest space together constitutes a Happy Ending. ⎯⎯ ⎯⎯

24. Unrequited love is better than no love at all. ⎯⎯ ⎯⎯

25. One of my favorite songs is "Only You"/ "Stand by Me"/ "I'd Rather Be Blind, Maimed, and Live in a Cardboard Box in Guatemala than Have to Spend Another Day without You." ⎯⎯ ⎯⎯

26. Sometimes he doesn't call for days on end. Well, for a month or two. But when he does show up he always brings me flowers and tells me how he can't live

without me. That's how I know that what
we have together is special.   ——   ——

27. You have been on a diet for thirty years.
Your husband is aware of this—how
could he not be when he's lived with you
for ten of those years, watching you
weigh the lettuce and exclaim over the
joys of existing on papaya and sunflower
seeds? Nonetheless, every Valentine's Day
your husband gives you a five-pound box
of chocolates. You don't think this shows
a lack of thought, sensitivity, or concern
for your hips. You think it's romantic.   ——   ——

28. The love of your life confesses to a
meaningless affair with a woman he works
with. (He confesses, primarily, because
you caught them necking in the parking
lot, but he assured you that guilt and
remorse were going to drive him to
confessing anyway; very soon.) To win
back your love and trust, he woos you as
once he wooed you when you were young
and took long walks in the rain together.
He buys you candy. He brings you flowers.
He takes you to dark restaurants where
you can't see what you're eating and holds
your hand over the ashtray. You can't help
but forgive. It's obvious that he can't live
without you.   ——   ——

29. If you'd been alive in the nineteenth
century and living in the Wild West—
and not a slave or a Native American,
in which case your options would have
been a little restricted—you would have

run off with a mysterious stranger dressed
all in black and wearing a mask first
chance you got.   ____   ____

30. When he says he'll phone and he doesn't,
I usually get through the first forty-eight
hours by imagining that he was hit by a
car on his way to my house and died on
the operating table calling my name, but
because of the anesthetic they thought
he was saying "Macaroons, get me
Macaroons."   ____   ____

31. You've been dating Y for five tumultuous
years. He is inaudibly handsome,
tragically unhappy, and a dedicated
loner. He never phones when he says
he'll phone. He forgets dates. He breaks
promises. The only time he gave you a
birthday present it wasn't your birthday,
it was his mother's. He got drunk the day
before your sister's wedding and turned
up in L.A. instead of at St. Andrew's in
Montgomery. You stay with him (if it
could be called staying)because you're
so in love with him.   ____   ____

32. If your boyfriend Damien, the rock
guitarist, were a rug he'd be floor-to-
ceiling carpeting in Madison Square
Garden, that's how much he lies. He lies
to you about money, other women,
where he's been, what he was doing
there, and what he did with your
grandmother's silver. The reason you
don't dump Damien for someone a bit
more reliable, not to say trustworthy

and less stressful, is that every time he
kisses you you go into meltdown. That
makes it all worthwhile.   ——— ———

33. Your best friend tells you a story that
    her sister's best friend's cousin told her.
    This is the story: The sister's best friend's
    cousin's brother was in Vietnam. While
    there, he fell in love with a beautiful
    Vietnamese girl. She fell in love with
    him. Amid the bombs and the napalm
    and the loud rock music, they planned
    the life they would have together back
    in Houston. Such are the fortunes of love
    and war, however, that he was wounded
    and sent home without seeing her again.
    When he could finally walk again, he
    went back to search for her, but she had
    vanished. Heartsick and devastated, he
    left Vietnam and his shattered dreams.
    Years later, on a business trip to San
    Francisco, he walked into a restaurant
    for lunch. As a sentimental gesture, he
    chose a Vietnamese restaurant. The
    waitress came over with the menu. He
    looked up. Their eyes met. It was his
    own true love. Two weeks later, they
    were married. Just thinking about this
    story cheers you up.   ——— ———

34. Just thinking about the above story
    cheers you up because not only do you
    believe every word of it, but you secretly
    think that the same thing will happen to
    you (not that you'll be bombed out of
    your home by the American army, but

Yes   No

that the person you're sure must have
been your own true love because you
haven't seen him in twenty years will
suddenly turn up on your doorstep with
an engagement ring and a bunch of red
roses).   ____ ____

35. Imagine this: You meet J at a wedding in
Boston. He is a friend of the groom's.
When you jump for the bridal bouquet,
it is on J that you land. After you help
him bandage his foot, the two of you
get to talking and you really hit it off.
You hit it off so well, in fact, that it
isn't long before you have determined
beyond a shadow of a doubt that his
teeth are capped and he has discovered
your fondness for garlic shrimp. After
the wedding, you return to Seattle and
he returns to Memphis. The next morning,
an enormous bouquet of flowers arrives
for you. "Hello from Tennessee" says the
card. You call J up to thank him. He says
he misses you. You say you miss him.
The next day he calls you. You call him
back that afternoon. Soon your phone
bill is equal to the national debt of
Bolivia and you are madly in love with
a man in whose company you've been
for a total of five hours, most of them
spent in a clinch in the cloakroom.
When J suggests that you sublet your
apartment, give up your job, and move
to Memphis to "see what happens" your
only question concerns the weather.   ____ ____

19

36. While on holiday in California, you fall madly in love with Daniel. Daniel has just broken up with his wife. He falls madly in love with you. You tear up your return ticket, give up your job back home, and move in with him. Two months later, Daniel tells you that all the while he's been with you, he's also been seeing his wife and though he cares very much about you they've decided on a reconciliation. You fail to inflict enough bodily harm on Daniel to do him any real damage and he moves back with his wife. Your dreams shattered, you decide to return to the safer shores of Maryland and beg for your old job and your old apartment back. You're still crying as you stagger toward the gate. Suddenly you hear someone shouting your name. You turn. It's Daniel. "Darling!" Daniel screams. "Darling! I've been a fool. Please don't go!" You drop your bags and hurl yourself into his strong, loving arms.   ——   ——

37. Love means never having to say you're sorry.   ——   ——

Any yes answer indicates a probable symptom of love addiction. Yes answers to several of the questions indicate the following stages of the disease:

1–12 yeses: Early stage (Apprentice Romantic).

13–24 yeses: Middle stage (Committed Romantic).

25–37 yeses: Beginning of the end (Sucker for Love).

Advice

My mother doesn't usually give advice, because, she claims, no one ever follows any of it. But she was asked to take part in a survey about men and why they're like that, and one of the questions concerned advice. The question was: If you had one piece of advice about men to give to a young girl just entering womanhood—something that would save her the years of stress and anxiety caused by making the same mistakes with men over and over again—what would it be?

"Shoot on sight," said my mother.

Advice From a Man

Men, as every woman knows, love to give advice. It makes them feel strong and useful. Needed. In control. The unfortunate thing about male advice, however, is that a man will as happily give you advice about things he knows nothing about as he will about things he knows something about. For this reason, you have to be very careful about soliciting advice from men, and even more cautious about following through on it. With one exception. And that is when the advice you need is about a man.

It works on the same principle as the native scout. Here you are this scrawny white person from some cramped and overpopulated city, all by yourself in the untamed wilderness, surrounded by people as different from you as moon men. It wouldn't matter if you could communicate with them, which you can't, because you wouldn't understand them anyway. So what do you do? Shuffle back home in defeat and resignation? No. You get yourself a friendly native to show you around. Your friendly native can explain the other, less friendly, natives to you. He can advise you on how to behave, what to expect, the significance of waking up one morning to find a dead toad hanging from the roof of your tent.

And so it is with men. If you go to your female friends with your problems about Nathan, your female friends will be warm, supportive, sympathetic, and full of practical, well-thought-out, intelligent advice based on all they have learned from painful experience about life, love, and human behavior. They'll bend over backward in their attempt to be both understanding and fair. "You have to try to imagine what Nathan's going through," they'll tell you. "You have to remember that this isn't easy for him. Maybe if you show him you trust him . . . maybe if you give him more room . . . maybe if you show him more attention . . . maybe if you let him know that you're not going to reject him for a few mistakes . . ."

But a man won't be handicapped by fairness and understanding.

A man will listen to Nathan's scheme for starting up his own business, and he'll say simply, "Don't lend him the money."

He'll listen to Nathan's reasons for buying fifty yard line Super Bowl tickets with the house insurance money and he'll say, "Take them back."

He'll drink three beers while you tell him about Nathan's reasons for having that fling in Acapulco, and then he'll say, "Dump him."

And why is the advice of a man always so much more simple than the advice you'll get from a woman? No, that's not why. It's because a man knows. He's a man, too. He knows that if you lend Nathan the money you'll never see it again. He knows that if you let Nathan keep the guitar he'll never play it. He knows that if you don't dump Nathan now you'll be dumping him several flings down the road.

Alien Nation

At the very root of the problem between the sexes is the fact that men and women only seem to come from the same planet and speak the same language. Because of certain superficial

22

physical characteristics, they give the appearance of being closely related, but in reality they no more belong to the same species than the blue-footed booby and the ground iguana.

Deep in their hearts, women know this. That's why women have a voice of exaggerated reasonableness and interest that they use only when speaking to small children or grown men. "Oh, really?" they say. "You feel a throbbing in your penis when you hear the first chord of 'Wild Thing'? Isn't that fascinating?"

That's why women talk about men to women differently than they talk about men to men. "Can you believe it?" they say to their girlfriends. "He actually spent forty-five minutes explaining the lyrics of 'Wild Thing' to me."

Men, however, do not know this. That is, they know that women are odd and don't act according to any logic they can figure out, but they think it must have something to do with menstruation. They don't realize it's because a lost spaceship containing the first men landed on this planet a million years ago. The men came from a distant galaxy. They'd intended to return to their own planet, but someone (possibly, legend has it, the wife of the captain) must have fiddled with the computer and they could never get the right coordinates again.

Attitude, Female

Many women acquire an ambiguous attitude about men as they grow older and have more experience with them. Where once they were rushing out to meet their princes with open arms, they suddenly become cautious. They want one, but they have learned not to trust them. They're fond of them, but, like someone who has lost a hand playing with a leopard, they shy from getting too close. They develop a tendency to laugh about men among themselves. They dither. They waver. They hedge their bets. Indeed, a person can become so wary that a prince riding up on a white charger would have to have a pretty hefty wad of character references and the Nobel Peace Prize in his possession before he could hope to get so much as a cup of tea. She wants to see the prince's star chart and speak to his old girlfriends before she'll consider a second date. She won't let him in to stay the night until she's interviewed his analyst and read his palm. Indeed, a few women develop such wariness that, Peace prize or no Peace prize, they'd shoot the poor bugger before he had a chance to dismount.

Men often mistake this defensiveness and sense of cautiousness for dislike and bitterness.

"What is it with women?" they want to know. "Why do they hate us? Are they all feminists? Women's libbers? Lesbians?"

Men can't understand why so many women should have an attitude about them. "What does it mean when they look at us like that?" they want to know. "What does it mean when they say, 'Oh, men!' and roll their eyes?"

It means they've fallen through one too many raised toilet seat in the middle of the night, that's what it means.

B

Being a Man

Being a man is like being an eagle or, indeed, a frog. No matter what the differences between individual men, there are certain attitudes and traits that all hold in common.

"You mean like worrying about your penis and lugging a cellular phone around with you all the time?" you ask.

That, too.

Recently I was awakened in the middle of the night by an ex-client of mine in a state of acute distress.

"Fran," I said, noting even in my sleepiness how upset she was. "Whatever's wrong?"

"Wrong?" wailed Fran. "Wrong? Ken's what's wrong, that's what's wrong."

"Come right over," I ordered.

While Fran was on her way over, I made some tea and composed myself as best I could. I was worried, I won't say I wasn't. Fran had gone cold turkey from Ken two years before, and, as far as I knew, had stopped showing any withdrawal symptoms months ago. Now here she was, calling me up in the middle of the night, hysterically wailing his name, just like she used to.

Fran arrived wearing a raincoat and a straw hat that said VIVA MEXICO, and carrying a considerable amount of luggage. "Ken!" she was screaming. "Ken Moped! I wished I'd killed you that night in Hartford when I had the chance."

"Fran," I said, trying not to sound critical. "Fran, did you go away on vacation with Ken?"

Fran threw herself into the nearest chair and her hat across the room. "No, of course I didn't, Dr. Gray," she said. "I went by myself. I've only just got back. I called you on my way from the airport."

"Then why are you so upset about Ken?" I asked. "Don't tell me he was in Mexico at the same time. Don't tell me you ran into him at the *aeropuerto*."

She shook her head. "It was the taxi driver," she informed me.

I set the tea on the table between us. "The taxi driver?" I started to pour. "You mean he looked like Ken?"

She shook her head a second time. "No, he looked nothing like Ken." Her tea cup rattled. "He was Ken!" she roared.

"I think that perhaps you ought to tell me what happened," I said.

Fran told me what happened.

She had not gone to Mexico on vacation since during the years she was with Ken they had never gone South of the Border because of Ken's feelings about foreigners and chili. She'd eaten a lot of chili, met a lot of foreigners, and had a wonderful time. She came back. Because of the late hour, she decided to take a taxi home. She got in the taxi. Not far from the airport, it became apparent that the taxi driver had no idea where they were going.

"Which road do I take now?" he kept asking her. "How much farther?" "Do I have to make a turn soon?"

Fran didn't know. "I think you can take the road we're on," she said, trying to be helpful, "but I'm not completely sure."

"Do you live in Brooklyn?" asked the driver.

Fran drank down her tea in one desperate swallow. "He had

that tone in his voice," said Fran. "You know the one I mean? The one that makes it sound like you probably don't know where you live?" I nodded. "Anyway," Fran continued, "then I said, 'Yes, I live in Brooklyn.' "

I gave us each another cup. "And what did he say?"

"He said, 'Then why don't you know the way from the airport?' "

I nodded.

"And I said, 'Because I've never driven to the airport from my home.' "

I stirred my tea slowly.

"And then he asked me if I could drive, and when I said yes he wanted to know why, if I could drive, I didn't know how to get from my home to the airport. 'You're supposed to know where you live,' he kept telling me. 'How can you not know?' " She practically threw the tea down her throat. "Finally I asked him why it was he didn't know how to get to my house from the airport when he was the taxi driver, and he accused me of having a negative attitude."

"I can see why he reminded you of Ken," I said.

"That's only the beginning," said Fran.

"The beginning?" I repeated.

She nodded. "You'd be amazed how many men I met in Mexico who reminded me of Ken."

"Not that amazed," I said.

Boy Talk

Jeff and Sylvia, the woman he has been living with for the past ten years, have just agreed to separate. It was a painful decision, and one that it took Jeff years to come to. After all, it wasn't as though he'd fallen madly in love with someone else and had no choice. It wasn't as if, his body taken over by his penis at a party one night, he'd been caught by Sylvia in an unforgivable act on

27

top of the coats. It wasn't even as though they fought all the time. Sylvia carried on a small guerrilla offensive of her own— that was, Sylvia was always thumping around muttering to herself and nagging him to pick up his socks or to do the dishes or to tell her what he really felt about his father—but aside from that their relationship was cordial, companionable, rather like that of a person and her/his dog.

Having finally made this difficult decision, however, Jeff realizes that he needs to discuss the situation and his feelings with another human being. Sylvia and he have been together for a long time. Like the car's regular oil change and his own six-month checkup at the dentist, she is part of the pattern of his life. To live without her is the emotional equivalent of suddenly finding yourself in one room in Barbados, unable to get the *TV Guide* or tortilla chips. He hasn't felt this terrified and disoriented since he spent that week in with his Canadian pen pal when he was twelve. The only person Jeff normally discusses anything of a personal nature with is Sylvia, but even he can see that this time she is not going to be willing to give him a sympathetic ear. So he invites his one friend, Ian, out for a drink. Ian's own life is a little on the emotionally fraught and complicated side at the moment as well. His son has dropped out of college and gone off to Nepal, his sixteen-year-old daughter is dating a man in his thirties, Ian himself, a science teacher, has just begun an affair with the new woman in his department, his mistress of four years is giving him a hard time about his promise to leave his wife when the children got older, and his wife gave him such a nice birthday last week that he thinks he may be falling in love with her again.

Jeff and Ian go for a drink and a little male interfacing.

JEFF: What'll you have?
IAN: A beer. [Jeff comes back to the table with a beer and a whiskey. Ian raises his mug to Jeff.] *Salud*.
JEFF: [sitting down] So, what's new?

IAN: [shrugs] Not much. [He sips his drink appreciatively.] The woman who replaced Norbert, Lisa?, she seems to be working out pretty well. She doesn't get along with Stoner either. She agrees with me that he's reactionary and out of touch with the students. She thought my idea for the senior projects was inspired.

JEFF: Oh yeah? What's she look like?

IAN: [shrugs] Her chin is too large, but otherwise she's not too bad. [He takes another drink.] What about you? Anything happening?

JEFF: [shrugs] Not much, you know. . . . I landed the Miller contract, which was a weight off my mind. And the new windshield wipers finally came.

IAN: [perking up] You going to put them on yourself or get the garage to do it?

JEFF: [who never for one second considered putting the windshield wipers on himself, not after what happened when he tried to put up that shelf in the bathroom] Oh, I'll do it myself. There's nothing to it really. [chugs back half his whiskey] Hear from Alexander lately?

IAN: We had a postcard. Alison's in a state, of course. You know what mothers are like. She's sure he's not eating right. "He's up a mountain," I told her. "He's not going to be getting three square meals a day up there, is he?"

JEFF: [laughs] Women always find something to worry about, don't they?

IAN: [also laughing] You can say that again. Now Alison wants to change the living room again. [He shakes his head.] Why is it that the minute you get the house in a comfortable state they want to change it around? Now she wants shutters.

JEFF: [glumly] Sylvia wanted shutters, too.

IAN: Really? How did you talk her out of them?

29

JEFF: [finishing off his drink] I told her I was moving out.

IAN: Really? And it worked?

JEFF: [nodding] I found a place this morning.

IAN: [puzzled] You mean you're really moving out?

JEFF: [largely to his drink] Uh-huh.

IAN: [thinking of how sweet Alison was when she took him out for his birthday and how Arlene keeps nagging him to tell Alison that he's leaving now that Alexander is up a mountain in Nepal and that Tina is getting it on with a man who could at least technically be her father, and how Lisa thinks everything he says and does is wonderful] How'd Sylvia take it?

JEFF: [shrugs] She's been crying a lot. You know what they're like.

IAN: [getting to his feet] My round.

Breaking the Habit

You've been seeing Sidney, the saxophone player, for nearly a year. When you and Sidney first started dating, you thought he was so wonderful you couldn't understand why he hadn't been cloned. Oh, sure, he had a few annoying traits (pathological lateness, a brunette named Donna) and one or two unappealing tendencies (debt, crying when drunk), but you ignored them. It won't interfere with us, you told yourself. It'll all work out in the end. Strangely enough, though, Sidney's traits and tendencies do interfere with you and him. Instead of working out in the end they make you crazy and drive you apart. You decide to end things with Sidney. You tell your friends. You tell your mother. You tell the woman in the dry cleaners and the guy in the liquor store. Everyone agrees with you. Sidney is a jerk. He's a nice-enough person in many ways—no one's saying that he isn't fun at parties or helpful at unclogging drains—but he has more problems than Dr. Ruth. "That's it, then," you say. "I am defi-

nitely breaking it off. Sidney and I are finished. Finito. Kaput."
You tell your hairdresser, the mailman, some friends who drop
in from New Zealand. You mention it to your father and your
dentist.

Who, of all the billions of people on this planet, don't you
tell? You don't tell Sidney.

Why don't you tell Sidney?

You don't tell Sidney because every time you start to tell him
he looks at you with those big brown eyes and you lose your
resolve. Because every time you start to tell him he does something sweet and endearing. Because every time you manage to
mumble a discouraging word he plays you "Moon River" on his
sax.

And nor is giving Sidney the old heave-ho the end of it. Usually it is only the beginning. No matter how great your relief to
be out of a relationship, it is never easy to let it go. There are
all the things you did together, all the places you went, all the
memories. You'll miss him. He'll miss you. He'll want to come
back. You'll want him to come. There'll be notes and postcards.
There'll be stilted, heart-wrenching phone calls—"Hi." "Hi."
"How are you?" "Fine. How are you?" "Oh, fine, just fine."—after
which you'll burst into tears. He'll call you to remind you about
having the oil burner serviced, and you'll call him to remind him
about the foot doctor. One stormy night there'll be a knock at
your door and Sidney will be standing there with the sick cat in
his arms—the cat you and he found among the garbage cans on
a night very much like this—and Sidney will be crying. You'll
invite him and Top Cat in. They'll stay the night. It won't be
until the morning, when Sidney borrows twenty dollars so he
can take the cat to the vet in a cab, that you'll begin to remember why you and Sidney broke up.

On the face of it, my mother, Althera Beryl Gray née Siracuso, and Neil Sedaka would seem to have little in common. My
mother doesn't sing, she was never a teen idol, and she has no
interest whatsoever in Las Vegas. Nonetheless, there is one thing

on which Althera Beryl Gray and Neil Sedaka are in total agreement, and that is when it comes to ending a relationship. "It's hard to do," Mrs. Gray and Mr. Sedaka agree.

"A relationship is like any other habit," says my mother. "You don't just wake up one morning and say, 'Hey, I don't think I'll drink coffee anymore.' It's part of the structure of your life. It's in your system. You like the way it makes the house smell. You like the sensation of that first mouthful every morning. The world would seem smaller and less friendly without it. You know that coffee isn't good for you, just as you know that that saxophone player you've been seeing isn't good for you, but neither of them is that easy to give up."

For this reason, my mother and I have come up with a twelve-step program for breaking the relationship habit, The Gray & Gray Twelve-step Love 'Em or Leave 'Em Recovery Program.

1. *Tell him goodbye.*

It'll never be over until you've made it clear that you'd rather be selling postcards in Atlantic City than doing anything with him. You may think this is something he should be able to figure out by himself, but it isn't.

"I don't really talk to him anymore," you say. "You know, not about real things. Surely he must know something's wrong."

Not necessarily and only if he's noticed.

"I listen to Patsy Kline and cry myself to sleep," you say. "Surely he must suspect that I'm unhappy."

He may just question your taste in music or think you're premenstrual.

"Okay, okay," you say, "but I've stopped sleeping with him. Now that's a hint he can't ignore."

Oh no, it isn't.

"All right then, I've been sneaking around town with a large German. How much more obvious can I get?"

Much more obvious. You have to put it into so many words. Don't wait for the right moment. Don't wonder if he'll ever be able to work the washing machine without you. Don't worry that you'll never find anyone better. Say it simply and say it quickly. Say, "Good-bye, Sidney." It helps if you've already packed his things and have them waiting in the hallway in a cardboard box. That way there can be no confusion. If you don't have his things ready to go, his initial response is likely to be, "What?" or "You don't mean 'goodbye,' do you?"

2. Be firm.

Sidney's second response—even if he came over to find his possessions scattered like leaves on the street outside your house—is likely to be anything from "You don't mean it" to "Are you sure?" Mean it. Be sure. Say, "Yes, I mean it, Sidney." Say, "Yes, I'm sure." When he says, "Why don't we sit down and talk it over?" say, "Because there's nothing to talk about." Which is probably true. If you have come this far you have already had all the arguments and discussions one couple need ever have. Don't have any more. He knows that he's selfish and insensitive. You know that you're bossy and don't understand him. Another eight months of hashing over just how selfish and how bossy aren't going to change anything. Hand him his box, open the door, and concentrate on repeating your best friend's phone number over and over in your head as Sidney walks slowly and sadly away. Don't look. The last thing you want is to meet the tear in his eye with the tear in your eye when he turns to gaze at you from the doorway.

3. Remember.

There are quite a few things about Sidney that you don't want to remember. The time he brought you vanilla fudge ice cream when you had that sore throat. The time he played "Only You" outside your office. The time he left a single red rose on every stair leading to your bedroom. Delete those files from your memory as quickly as you can. What you want to remember are all the things about Sidney that make you want to break his neck. Remember the way he eats soup.

How nervous he used to get when you drove his car. His habit of correcting you in front of other people. Remember every unkind thing he ever said about your family, your cats, your taste in clothes, food or literature; recall every crack he ever made about Willie Nelson or Johann Sebastian Bach. If Sidney had an affair with someone else while you were together, imagine him kissing her at the same time that you were making his favorite meal. Whatever you do, don't forget the time he woke you at four in the morning to tell you that your breathing was annoying him.

4. Blame him.

Even if everything that went wrong was your fault—which is impossible, only 50 percent could ever be blamed on you—don't blame yourself, blame him. Don't start feeling guilty now. Guilt, like hope, destroys your peace of mind. And, also like hope, guilt is a major waste of time. So there were things you could have done that you didn't do. There always are. You didn't do them, and you can't go back and do them now. So there were things you did do that you shouldn't have done. There are always those things too.

When you find yourself leaning against the kitchen counter, eating dry cereal out of the box, and thinking about the time you refused to iron a shirt for him or lend him the money for his insurance, remind yourself that you would have been far more generous, giving, tolerant, and understanding if Sidney hadn't been such a jerk.

When you realize that you're standing in front of the dairy case, staring vacantly at the artificial cream and wishing you had never had that affair with the Armenian, keeping in mind that you wouldn't have had that affair with the Armenian if you hadn't been so fed up with Sidney.

5. Stomp on hope.

Where most people go wrong when they're trying to get over someone is by maintaining the tiny candle of hope flickering faintly deep in their hearts. You've told Sidney to go, you've packed his bags, Sidney's gone, and then you find yourself sitting in the bathtub wondering if you haven't been a little hasty. Maybe he could change, you say to yourself. Maybe he does really care.

You start going over every word Sidney has ever said and everything he has ever done, and you reinterpret them in a more favorable light. When Sidney said, "I don't want a permanent relationship" maybe he didn't mean he never wanted a permanent relationship, or that he didn't want a permanent relationship with you. Maybe what he meant was that he didn't want a permanent relationship now. When Sidney didn't turn up for your birthday maybe it wasn't because he has so little feeling for you that he couldn't even be bothered to miss softball practice, maybe it was because he genuinely forgot.

Eliminate hope. Hope is a killer. Hope keeps you marching into places where not only angels but fools fear to tread. Any one of your friends could (and probably have) told you that Sidney is a Neanderthal who will never make it to the bronze age, but you won't believe them. You keep telling yourself that he can be trained to eat cooked foods and use a fork. He can't. Even if you get him in a suit and sitting at the table, the minute he smells blood he'll be off again. Once you've accepted the fact that Sidney is not going to change—not ever, not never, no matter what, and definitely not with you—then you can get on with your life.

6. *Pretend he's dead.*

The Better-Dead-Than-in-Montana Method is the surest way of stomping on hope once and for all. If you don't think of him as dead but hang on to the fact that he is alive and well and probably happy as a compulsive eater at a barbecue in Dallas, there's always the risk that you'll begin thinking of him again. You'll wonder if you'll ever run into him; if time might change things; what he's doing; who he's with; what he's saying about you.

It was actually my mother who developed the BDTM technique after her first husband ran off to Guatemala to save the Third World.

"I was devastated," she recalls. "I'd trusted that man completely. We were crazy about each other. I would've been less surprised to wake up in the morning and find that the sun had turned blue than I was to find that note on my pillow." My mother cried for days. She shuffled around the house in her bathrobe, imagining what Turnbull was doing while she was cleaning the toilet bowl with a toothbrush. She couldn't get over the habit of talking to him in her head. She told him about the fight with the milkman, she told him about the documentary on walruses, she asked his opinion on dying her hair. Every time the phone rang she jumped, thinking it might be him. Every time the mail came through the door she strolled slowly and casually into the hall to pick up the letters that never arrived. She imagined scenes in which, years in the future, she was queen of England and married to Sean Connery and she ran into Turnbull in a waterfront bar and he begged her to take him back. She laughed.

"I was driving myself insane," says my mother. "I knew that if I didn't do something drastic and final I might spend the rest of my life obsessed with a man who was living in a cardboard box and singing 'Guantanamera' in broken Spanish."

So my mother decided to act as if Turnbull were dead. He's dead, she told herself. You'll have to come to terms with that. She told friends and acquaintances and people she met on public transportation. "He was perfect," she told them. "We were very much in love. And then, only a week before our first anniversary, he was tragically run over by a bus. Outside of Woolworth's."

It worked like a charm.

7. *Talk about him.*

Men hate to think that after you've broken up with them you go around telling all your friends what dorks they were.

"Just do me one favor," Sidney says to you as he's slinking out the door. "Don't tell Daisy about the bill I ran up on your credit card. I have my pride, you know." This, in fact, was something that you didn't know. You stare at him blankly. "Just tell her that our separation was by mutual agreement," says Sidney.

Stuff that for a turkey, is what I say. Tell Daisy and everybody else you know about the credit card. Tell them about the time you came home to find him wearing your bathing suit. Call up the international operator and tell her. Stop strangers of the street to tell them. When you go to dinner parties, recount the story of Sidney getting so jealous of your best friend that he chased her out of the house with the garden spade. Make sure everyone Sidney knows has heard about the food fight in the Italian restaurant. The more you talk about him, the better you'll feel. Not only that, but if you tell enough people what a waste of your time Sidney was, it'll help to keep both guilt and hope at bay. Having stoop up on Oprah and told the entire planet about Sidney throwing a plate of lasagne at the plastics salesman from Düsseldorf you can't very well take him back now.

8. *Remind yourself of your differences.*

When you're involved with someone it's easy to see how ill-suited you are for one another. Every time he gives you that You're-not-really-putting-mustard-on-your salad? look or sighs when you start explaining what happened to the kettle, you are reaffirmed again in your knowledge that this is not the man for you. You have nothing in common. You disagree on politics, movies, music, books, and the restorative powers of double-cheese burritos. You love to travel and he thinks taking the bus into town is a major journey. His idea of uncontrollable passion is to hold your hand in public. But when he's taken his things and gone to sleep on some friend's sofa you start feeling differently. All of a sudden you miss the sight of all his vitamins lined up in the medicine chest. When you brush your hair in front of the bathroom mirror you long for the sound of Sidney screaming, "How many times do I have to tell you, you're going to clog up the drain!" The house feels silent without the noise of Sidney singing along to Lionel Richie. Sidney and I both liked hot curries, you hear yourself saying. We were both born in June. We both like red and Stephen King. We've both been to New Orleans. We really have so much in common.

That's why it's so important to take time each day to go through all the things that separated you and Sidney. Do this instead of your morning workout or your midmorning coffee break. He always wears a suit and you always wear jeans. He likes pizza and you're allergic to wheat. You love the beach and he starts sweating when the heating goes on. He can't sleep if he's had a cup of coffee less than six hours before bedtime and you live on caffeine. He never drinks more than two glasses of wine and you throw out the cork as soon as you open the bottle. He reads Jeffrey Archer. By the time you reach the point in your list where he hates your best friend and thinks you should make the cat sleep outside you'll be back in the mood to break his neck.

9. *Make a list of Sidney's best lines and tape it to the refrigerator door.*
The beauty of this is that not only are you reminded of all the dumb things Sidney said to you every time you reach for a yogurt or a bottle of beer, but you have the chance of reliving your initial reaction whenever one of your friends reads the list. "What's this?" says your friend, moving the chocolate chip cookie magnet out of the way. " 'How can you tell the woman you love that you can't live with her?' " Your friend starts to giggle. "Who said that?" he wants to know. You tell him it was Sidney. He goes back to the list. " 'No matter what happens, I'll always value your friendship,' " he reads, spluttering with laughter. "Good grief, Sidney didn't say that to you, did he?" You nod. "And he's still alive?" shrieks your friend. You nod. " 'Being with me has made you boring.' Sid-

ney?" he gasps. "Sidney said that?!" You smile. " 'You're almost my intellectual equal.' " Howls of laughter rock the entire apartment. "Sidney," you say.

10. *Spend time with couples.*

Many experts would advise you to avoid couples at this difficult period, in case it makes you feel left out and rejected. But my mother and I agree that unless you are the only person in the galaxy who knows only couples in the first throes of being madly in love, spending time with couples is a good way of reminding yourself exactly what you're missing. The petty squabbles over food and toothpaste, the snide remarks about each other's friends, the cracks about putting on weight and going bald. Think about it. Think about what playing Scrabble with Andy and Gina is like. He takes forty minutes every turn and won't let you give Gina any help, and she always winds up knocking the board off the table. By the time you've sat through an evening with Andy and Gina, you'll never want to be in a relationship again.

11. *Count.*

Count all the things you can do without Sidney that you could never do with him. Get up as early as you like. Go to bed as late as you want. Eat peanut-butter-and-cheese sandwiches without being made an object of ridicule. Leave your shoes in the hall. Bring germs into the house. Hang your stockings in the bathroom. Listen to Peruvian flute music at three in the morning. Go out with your friends whenever you want. Have your friends over whenever you want. Talk on the telephone for an hour without a short, balding men carrying a sign that says DO YOU KNOW WHAT THIS IS COSTING PER MINUTE? walking past the living-room door.

Count all the things that you had to do with Sidney that you no longer have to do. Have Sunday lunch with his parents. Go to football games. Sit on a pier while Sidney spends Saturday putting dead things on his hook and yelling at you not to make too much noise. Watch television. Play Trivial Pursuit. Pretend to like Crystal Gale.

12. *Find someone new.*

Coming off a man is like coming off drugs. During those first difficult months without Sidney you will experience severe withdrawal symptoms. You'll feel a pang every time you walk into the bathroom and see the space in the holder where his toothbrush used to be and the space on the floor where he always left his socks. You'll find it difficult to drive without Sidney sitting beside you, telling you what you're doing wrong and squeaking on the turns. You'll want to cry every time you're in a bad mood and there's no Sidney there to ask you if you're premenstrual. Indeed, months after Sidney's departure, you'll undoubtedly still find yourself sitting on the bus, arguing with him about the time he fell asleep in the movie house and was six hours late for your birthday party.

Obviously, you must do something to get your thoughts on something else as quickly as possible, but what?

Many experts recommend taking up a hobby or finding a new interest. Rug-hooking, they suggest. Pottery. Investigating the history of glass-making—that'll get your mind off Sidney. Others favor a busy social life as the best distraction from the longings and homicidal dreams associated with the end of an affair. Get out, they say. See people. Do things. Enjoy yourself. Have a good time.

But of all the positive things you can do during this difficult period, personal experience has proven that nothing is nearly as effective as seeing another man. Seeing another man will take your mind off Sidney in a way that needlework classes and Japanese film festivals never could.

Instead of spending all your free time remembering all the annoying things Sidney did, you will soon discover that you're spending all your free time being annoyed by somebody new. Somebody who isn't Sidney will be correcting your pronunciation and the way you boil water. Somebody who isn't Sidney will be taking you to tennis matches to try to convince you that you're wrong about how boring they are. Somebody who isn't Sidney will be leaving his dirty dishes in the sink and asking you where the corkscrew is.

Before you know it, one evening when the aroma of Sidney's miso soup still lingers at the back of your fridge, you'll find yourself having the following telephone conversation with your best friend:

"And did I tell you what I found out last night?"

"Oh, my God," your best friend gasps. "He's not a cross-dresser like that psychiatrist I dated in 'eighty-nine, is he?"

"This is even weirder," you assure her. "You're not going to believe it. You're just not going to believe it."

"Are small animals involved?" she asks.

"Wait for it," you say. You pause dramatically. You take a deep breath. "I found out that he took the lawn with him when he moved!" you tell her. "What do you think of that? He took the lawn with him, even the crabgrass! Dug the whole thing up, blade by blade."

"Sidney?" your best friend asks in a horrified whisper. "Sidney took the lawn with him when he moved?"

"Sidney?" you'll reply. "Where did Stanley come from? I'm talking about John."

C

Change. Can He? Can You?

Many people will argue that my mother was wrong to go around Great Neck telling everyone that Woolworth's sent a special wreath in the company colors to Jack Turnbull's funeral, the thought of which, to this day, makes her cry. They will say that if she had been a little more flexible and forgiving and had taken Turnbull back when he begged her two years later, everything would have been different.

"Newt manure," says my mother. "People change slower than rocks." Imagine a couple. We'll call them Brent and Candy. After a long and often tumultuous relationship, Brent and Candy finally broke up after Brent drove his Volkswagen through Candy's living room because he thought she was seeing someone else.

"That does it, Brent," Candy told him. "I loathe you. You give toe cheese a bad name. From now on, Brent Collier, you are history."

Candy had had enough. After all the fights and tears and slammed doors; after all the times she'd stormed from the house at three in the morning to drive around town, crying while Willie Nelson sang on the tape deck, Candace Starsky was free at last. She vowed she would never speak to Brent again so long as she lived. Brent agreed.

"I understand your anger," said Brent, wiping away the tears. "I'm a bastard. You're better off without me. I'll never darken your door again."

What happens next?

"Candy and Brent never see each other again?" you suggest.

It's a guess.

What happens is that a few days, or a few weeks, or a few months pass, and Brent begins to darken Candy's telephone. "I was thinking about you," he says, his voice not shrill, as it is when he is accusing Candy of flirting with the mailman or sneaking junk food into the house, but soft and concerned. "So I just thought I'd call and see how you are."

"I'm fine," says Candy in a tight, flat voice.

"How's the cat?" asks Brent.

"Fine," says Candy.

After that first phone call, there are others. Every week or so Brent calls to make sure that nothing awful has happened to Candy or her cat. Candy becomes less frosty as the weeks go by. Instead of saying "Fine" she starts telling him how the cat got stuck in the washing machine and the adventure she herself had when the satellite dish fell off the roof. They laugh together, just as they used to laugh together when they weren't hurling pots and cutlery at one another's head. Candy starts remembering all the things about Brent that she used to love. The good times haunt her like a particularly determined ghost. He's not such a bad guy, Candy says to herself. Brent asks her to go to see that new Icelandic movie that's on at the art center, since no one else he knows would enjoy it. Candy goes. Candy asks Brent to go for a meal with her at a funky Afro-Canadian café she's heard about that no one else she knows will try. Brent goes. They start reminiscing about all they've done together besides try to kill one another. The next thing you know, Candy's asking Brent to move back in.

"Are you nuts?" shout Candy's friends. "You know what he's like. He's one rung below the saber-toothed tiger on the evolutionary ladder."

"He's changed," says Candy. "He's different now."

"Oh, sure," say her friends. "And they're wearing overcoats in hell."

Brent moves back in. That is, Brent moves back in until the night he throws all her clothes, jewelry, and her Elvis collection out on the street in a jealous rage. Then he moves out again. For three months, this time. The next time he moves out for a week. The next time for nearly a year. The next time for six months and a day. Because of this inability to separate, neither Brent nor Candy ever finds a new partner, and eventually they marry because it seems like the logical thing to do. It lasts six months. Candy's still wondering whether or not to take Brent back.

Communication Between the Sexes

A Case Study

Roger and Anne came to see me one grizzly autumn about a problem they, as a couple, were having communicating with one another.

"He doesn't," was how Anne put it. She shot Roger a Don't-pretend-you-don't-know-what-I'm-talking-about look and leaned toward me. "He tells me nothing," she said. "Nothing at all. I might as well be living with primitive man and not a vice president with a degree in philosophy."

Roger mumbled something.

"What?" I asked.

Roger stared at the corner of my desk. "It's not that I don't tell her anything," said Roger. "It's that she overreacts to everything I do tell her."

Anne raised an eyebrow. "Are we talking about the car?" Before Roger could answer, she turned back to me. "Last week I

44

came out of the house with the baby and the stroller and a box of old clothes I was taking to the church for the rummage sale, and some guy was driving my car away. So, naturally, I reported it stolen."

I leaned toward her. "Tell me," I said. "Did the police officer who took your call make you feel like it was your fault?"

She made a face. "Did he! First he suggested that I had forgotten where I parked the car. Then he insinuated that I'd parked illegally and the car had been towed."

"That's exactly what happened to me!" I cried.

"Yes, but your car really was stolen, wasn't it?" asked Anne. She gave Roger another look.

"And yours wasn't?"

Anne shook her head. "No," she said flatly. "It had been repossessed."

"Repossessed?"

Both of us looked at Roger. Roger shrugged.

"Yes," said Anne. "Repossessed."

"Roger," I said. "Roger, is this true? Did you know that the car was going to be repossessed, and you didn't tell your wife?"

Roger stared at his shoes. "I didn't want to upset her," he said.

Anne laughed, hollowly. "Like chasing your car for two blocks with a baby crying in your arms isn't upsetting." She jabbed him in the ribs. "Tell Dr. Gray why the car was repossessed," she ordered. "Go on." She glanced at me. "You're going to love this," she assured me. "It's classic."

Roger looked at the floor. "The car was repossessed because I couldn't keep up the payments."

I nodded encouragingly. "Yes . . . ?"

"Go on," urged Anne. "Tell her why you couldn't keep up the payments."

Roger studied a bit of fluff on the carpet. "Because I lost my job."

I looked from him to Anne and back again. "Are you saying that you lost your job and you didn't tell your wife?"

Roger nodded.

Anne made the sound of a Jack Russell terrier sticking its nose down a hole.

"Why not?" I persisted.

Roger looked at the side of my desk. "I didn't want her to worry."

Anne jabbed him again. "Tell her," she said. "Tell Dr. Gray how long it was before I found out that you were unemployed."

Roger looked at her as though her eyes had turned orange. "But you just told her," he said. "You found out when the car was repossessed."

"Tell her in numbers," said Anne.

Roger shrugged. "Six months."

"Six months?" I turned to Anne. "I know he's quiet," I said, "but you must have noticed him hanging around the house."

"He wasn't hanging around the house," she explained. "He was going to work every day."

We both looked at Roger. He shrugged again.

"Let me get this straight," I said. "You pretended to go to work every day for six months when in reality you had no work to go to? Just so you wouldn't have to tell your wife you'd lost your job?"

"That's right," said Anne. She shook her head. "Every morning he put on his suit, picked up his attaché case and his cellular phone, and he drove into the city."

"If you knew how emotional she is—" began Roger.

Feeling a little emotional myself, I cut him off. "But what did you do all day?" I asked. "Where did you go?"

Roger contemplated his knee. "I went to the library."

Anne rolled her eyes. "Where else?"

D

Did You Give Me the Right Key?

"But what'd I do?" wailed Mandrake. "All I said to her was, 'Are you sure you gave me the right key, honey?' and the woman went nuts." He touched his cheek, down which ran the scratches made by several door keys being pulled hard. "Let me tell you what happened," he said.

Mandrake told me what happened. His girlfriend, Bess, had called him up in a bit of a panic because the front door was jammed and she'd been having trouble getting in over the past few days. It had gotten so bad that she was afraid to leave the apartment in case she couldn't get back in. "Don't panic," Mandrake told her. "I'll be right over."

Mandrake went right over. "Give me the key," he said to Bess. Bess gave him the key. He tried it in the lock. It didn't work. He tried it again. It still didn't work. He fiddled it back and forth. Nothing. That was when he turned to Bess and said, "Are you sure you gave me the right key, honey?" and she tried to remove half his face with the Yales.

His story done, Mandrake looked at me with the baffled expression many men assume after an encounter with a female, especially one whom they know well. "What got her so mad?" he asked. "I didn't do anything, did I?"

"Well, yes and no," I said.

Don't Tell Your Father

The first piece of wisdom I remember learning at Beryl Gray's knee was, "Don't tell your father."

My father was away on business and my mother and I were eating pizza in the living room and wearing our shoes in the house. My father believed that pizza kills, he wouldn't allow food outside of the kitchen (because, unlike food inside the kitchen, it might attract insects), and he was allergic to the smell of shoe leather.

"Why not Mommy," I asked, curious, pulling mozzarella off the sofa.

"Because he'll just make a big deal out of it," said my mother.

From that moment on I understood that there are always things that the women surrounding a man don't tell him. Sometimes these things are minor—like letting leather into the house when he's not around—and sometimes they are major—like not mentioning to the man who thinks of you as fragile and innocent that you once ran guns for the CIA. Men think this is because women are in a conspiracy against them, but that isn't why. It's because there are so many things that men can't or won't handle. And because they hate anything that interferes with the way they do things, see things, or want things to be. It is not a conspiracy against them. It is a conspiracy to have as peaceful a life as possible in spite of them.

For instance, you know that if you suggest to Z that you would like to go away by yourself for a few days he will become disgruntled. Without me? he'll squawk. Pointing out that he has often gone away without you won't convince him. Reminding him that you're paying won't mollify him. Why can't I come? he'll want to know. What started out as a spur-of-the-moment whim will turn into a major two-month argument that incorporates every argument you have ever had in the past, and in the end you either won't go or you'll go and come back the same day because you feel so guilty.

So what do you do? You tell him your mother needs to get away for a few days. "Don't think I'm coming along," he'll say, diving behind his paper. "You're on your own for that one."

Driving to the Draculas

A Dramatization

It is a sunny autumn afternoon. Martha and Edward are on their way to spend the weekend with the Draculas at their new home in the country. It is a long drive into unfamiliar territory (at least three hours from their home, not including stops for coffee and the restroom), but Martha and Edward are equipped with minutely detailed directions from Alan Dracula, who is something of an expert on shortcuts in the countryside. When we join Martha and Edward, they have already been on the road for five hours and haven't spoken for the last one and a half. This is because of a series of arguments that started with the one over how often Martha made Edward stop so she could use the restroom ("Rest!" Edward shouted. "You might as well move in!" "I can't help it if I have to go to the toilet, Edward. I'm only human, you know," said Martha) and ended with the one about why they couldn't stay on the highway and follow the AAA route ("Because the AAA route is for people who don't love the open road the way Alan and I love the open road, Martha, that's why. The AAA route is for peasants.").

MARTHA: You and your shortcuts.
EDWARD: Umph.
MARTHA: [looking from the maps and papers on her lap to the tree-lined road in front of them] Edward, I really think we should stop and—

EDWARD: [groaning] Don't tell me you have to go to the toilet again.

MARTHA: —ask for directions.

EDWARD: [reaching over and thumping the papers Martha is
holding] We have directions, Martha. We have
directions from the roadmaster who devised the
quickest back-roads route from Chevy Chase to
Caribou.

MARTHA: [sounding more than doubtful] But I'm not sure
we're going the right way, Edward. I thi-

EDWARD: We're going the right way.

MARTHA: [frowning at the passing fields and trees and occasional warm-blooded animal] I really think we—

EDWARD: For the last time, Martha, I know where we are.

MARTHA: [turning in her seat for a glimpse of a road sign] But
where are we, Edward? I don't think—

EDWARD: [with exaggerated patience] We're on the road to
Little Falls, Martha, that's where we are. Just as
we're meant to be. [He leans over and thumps
the directions again.] If you spent half as much
time navigating as you do looking for a toilet
you'd know that.

MARTHA: Are you sure? [She peers at the map drawn by Alan
Dracula.]

EDWARD: [sighing] What did Alan say, Martha? He said to
make the right turn at the gas station. We made
the right turn. He said we'd pass an old church
three-quarters of a mile later. Three-quarters of a
mile later we passed an old church. . . .

MARTHA: [still peering at Alan Dracula's cartographic endeav-
ors] But maybe it wasn't the right gas station,
Edward. And maybe it wasn't the right old
church. We've passed so many. . . .

EDWARD: What's that supposed to mean, Martha? Is that
another sarcastic crack about leaving the high-

way? [He addresses the roof of the car.] I have to be married to the only person in the world who would rather look at Pizza Huts than the glorious New England countryside.

MARTHA: [squinting at Alan Dracula's densely written directions] I would not rather look at Pizza Huts than the glorious New England countryside, Edward, but I don't want to spend the entire weekend lost in the glorious New England countryside.

EDWARD: [coming dangerously close to the countryside in question] We're not lost, Martha.

MARTHA: [rattling road maps] Okay, we're not lost, Edward. But I would like to get to the Draculas' before it's time to turn around and go home again.

EDWARD: [sighing] We are on the road to Little Falls, Martha, all right? [He gives her a look as they bounce through a few ruts in the road.] You just keep your eyes peeled for our next turn. [He accelerates slightly; something falls off the back.] Maybe this time you won't wait till we've passed it to tell me where it is.

MARTHA: [banging her head on the windshield as she attempts to read a rapidly passing road sign] But how do you know we're on the road to Little Falls, Edward? There haven't been any si-

EDWARD: Trust me, Martha. Trust Alan. [sighs again] Not only do we have the directions of an expert to go on, but you seem to forget that I grew up in this part of the country, Martha. I do know my way around. It's in my blood.

MARTHA: But I haven't seen any—

EDWARD: What is it, Martha? Do you want to drive? Is that it, Martha? Would the woman who cries whenever she comes to an intersection like to take the wheel?

MARTHA: No, Edward, I don't want to take the wheel. I just
think that maybe we should stop and ask—
EDWARD: I don't need to ask, Martha. I know where I'm going.
MARTHA: Well do you think we could stop somewhere that
has a toilet?

Two hours later, dusk is falling over the glorious New England
countryside. Martha and Edward are stopped in some bushes by
the side of the road while a herd of cows stroll by on their way
home. Edward is studying Alan Dracula's directions while
Martha looks at the AAA map.

MARTHA: You know something, Edward. I'm not so sure we
should have crossed the bridge back there.
EDWARD: Umph.
MARTHA: [frowning as she traces the map with her finger] As
far as I can tell from this, we shouldn't have been
anywhere near that bridge.
EDWARD: [reading from Alan Dracula's directions] "After you
pass through Dogsbower, cross the Stillwater
Bridge and continue for a mile and two-thirds
until you come to a lightning-damaged oak tree
just inside an eighteenth-century stone fence.
Take the second left." [He thumps the paper
against the steering wheel, accidentally setting
off the horn, which causes a largish domestic
bovine animal to crash into the side mirror.] Are
you saying that you know the way better than
Alan, Martha? Is that what you're saying? That
you know the way better than the man with the
national record for getting from New York City
to Sesame, Georgia, without ever touching a
major highway?
MARTHA: No, Edward, I'm not saying that. I'm just saying
that I think we should ask—

EDWARD: I don't need to ask, Martha. I know where we are. [He jabs at Alan's map, which looks, in the gathering gloom, more like the scribbles of a four-year-old than the work of the nation's leading roadmaster, and lets loose an excited cry.] I've got it! See here, Martha? See where we went wrong? You told me to go right by that clump of holly bushes, but it was the second right we should have taken.

MARTHA: [as the last cow and its escort plod past the car] Maybe if we just ask this young woman—

EDWARD: We don't need to ask. [starting the engine] We'll be there in thirty minutes, Martha. Mark my words.

MARTHA: [mumbles something about needing a toilet]

Later the same night. The moon looks like a sliver of lemon hooked on the rim of a deep black cup and the stars are faint and far away. Nightbirds chatter and something in the distance howls. Edward, parked in a field, rereads Alan Dracula's directions by the light of a flashlight. By the light of another flashlight, Martha approaches across the cow pats.

MARTHA: [getting back into the car] I don't believe it, squatting in the bushes in the dark at my age. I'm lucky I wasn't bitten by a snake or something.

EDWARD: There are no poisonous snakes in New England, Martha. Why do you women always have to exaggerate so?

MARTHA: [slamming the door shut] And why do you men always have to think you're right? [She folds her arms across her lap and stares through the windshield at the rather surreal landscape of the glorious New England countryside at night.] If you'd just stopped and asked for some help at the start—

EDWARD: Help, Martha? [He shakes Alan Dracula's map and directions at her.] There you go again, undermining me . . . criticizing . . . nagging. . . . I don't need help, Martha. I need a navigator who can read English, that's what I need. A navigator who doesn't spend most of the trip in the toilet!

MARTHA: [through gritted teeth as she pulls a piece of shrubbery out of her shoe] Why can't you admit it, Edward? Why can't you just say, "You're right, Martha, we're lost"? Huh, Edward? Why can't you just own up to the fact that you've screwed up and we have to go back along the main road until we find someone we can ask for directions?

EDWARD: [ceremoniously folding up the map and the directions and placing them on the dash] Because we're not lost, Martha, that's why. You think we're in this field because I don't know where we are, but we're not. For the last time, we are not lost.

MARTHA: Edward, even if we just find a phone and call the Dracu-

EDWARD: We're in this field because you had to go to the toilet for the four-hundredth time today, Martha. That's why we're in this field. I happen to know exactly where we are. I have never been lost in my life. [He turns the key in the ignition.] And now, if you don't have to powder your nose or touch up your lipstick or urinate again, we'll just be on our way. [The engine splutters and then dies.]

MARTHA: [looks over] What's wrong?

EDWARD: [trying to start the engine again, but without even a splutter this time] Nothing's wrong, Martha. She's just a little cold, that's all. From waiting so long for you.

MARTHA: We're out of gas, aren't we?

EDWARD: I told you, Martha, we're not out of gas. The engine's a little cold—that's all.

MARTHA: [leaning toward the driver's side] I knew it! We're out of gas.

EDWARD: We're not out of gas, Martha. That gauge has never been right since you took the car to that garage—

MARTHA: Don't start about the garage again, Edward. There was nothing wrong with that garage. [opens the door]

EDWARD: [still trying to start the car] Now where are you going?

MARTHA: Since we're obviously going to be here for a while, I'm going to the toilet.

Thought Questions:

1. Why is Alan Dracula obsessed with travel routes?

2. Why won't Edward admit that he and Martha are lost?

3. Why didn't Martha insist on driving?

4. Why does she spend so much time in the toilet?

The Egg Argument

If Romeo and Juliet hadn't had the good fortune to die before they had a chance to move in together and really get to know one another, they, like most couples, would eventually have found themselves embroiled in the egg argument.

The egg argument?

Yes, the egg argument. Otherwise known as the three-hour heated discussion on the right way to boil an egg. Here's how it goes.

One morning Romeo comes down to breakfast, much as usual. He's a little grumpy because he couldn't find any clean socks and Juliet washed his Jockies with something red, turning them pink, and she's using his razor again, even though he's told her about a million times not to go near it.

Juliet, whizzing around the kitchen feeding the kids, and the cats, and the dog, and making the school lunches, and trying to put her makeup on at the same time, smiles as Romeo stomps into the room. "Good morning, sweetie," she calls.

Romeo removes a small shoe and a hunk of chewed banana from his chair and sits down. "Umph," says Romeo.

"How about a boiled egg and toast?" asks Juliet.

"Three minutes, not four," says Romeo, sniffing the orange juice before pouring himself a glass.

"Of course, darling," says Juliet. "How could I forget?"

Normally, Romeo reads his paper while Juliet boils his egg, but this morning a small Capulet has soaked his paper with milk and soggy cornflakes, so instead he watches the love of his life as she prepares his breakfast. He watches her fill the pan with water. He watches her put the egg in the pan. He watches her put the pan on the stove.

"Juliet, love," says Romeo. "Juliet, what are you doing?"

Juliet glances over her shoulder. She smiles. "I'm boiling an egg," she says, in her simple way.

"Like that?" asks her beloved.

The smile solidifies on her lovely face. "Like what?"

Romeo nods toward the pan with the water and the egg in it that she has just placed on the burner. "Like that."

Juliet looks at the pan. "Like what?" she asks again.

"Darling," says the light of her life. "Darling, one doesn't boil an egg that way."

Juliet turns back to him. She is still smiling. "This is the way I always boil eggs," she says sweetly. "I've been boiling eggs this way for a good many years."

"But it's wrong," says the holder of her heart. "One brings the water to a boil first, and then one puts the egg in. How else will you know that you've cooked it for precisely three minutes?"

Juliet pulls a loose strand of her hair in a way he once found both titillating and endearing, but that now rather gets on his nerves. "One knows that it's cooked for precisely three minutes because one times it as soon as the water starts to boil," she says.

Romeo laughs, a sound that was once like music to Juliet's ears but that is now more reminiscent of the croak of a frog. "But, sweetheart," he says. "Surely you can see how illogical that is. The water has been heating up for several minutes already. Ergo, the egg has already begun to cook. Ergo, it is not a three-minute egg."

"But the egg doesn't start cooking until the water boils, darling," says she. "Ergo, it is a three-minute egg." She reaches over and slaps a tiny Capulet on the head. "And besides, if you put the egg into boiling water it will crack."

"Not if you're careful, it won't," says Romeo, whacking a very small Capulet hand. "Not if you put enough salt in the water."

Time passes. Several eggs have been hard-boiled and several Capulets have been smacked by one or both of their parents, and still Romeo and Juliet are at it hammer and tongs. Voices are raised. By now, there are cookbooks all over the kitchen table. Some recommend putting the egg in boiling water; some recommend putting the egg in cold water and bringing it to a boil.

"Don't you see?" screams Juliet. "It doesn't matter. Who cares which way you boil an egg?"

"I couldn't expect you to care," says Romeo. "Not someone with your temperament and shaky grasp of logic. But I care. There's a right way to do things and there's a wrong."

Juliet bursts into tears. "I can't believe this," she sobs. "I can't believe I'm having an argument about how to boil an egg!"

"And I can't believe you insist on doing it wrong!" screams the center of her universe.

At her wit's end, Juliet reaches for the phone.

"What are you doing now?" asks Romeo.

"I'm calling your mother," says Juliet. "I'm going to ask her how she boils eggs. I'd call my mother, but I know you wouldn't listen to her."

Juliet calls Mrs. Capulet. She explains the egg argument. At the end of her tearful story, Mrs. Capulet sighs. "Well, honey," says Mrs. Capulet, "I used to boil eggs the way you do. But Mr. Capulet won't let me do it like that anymore."

Everywoman's Questionnaire

Despite centuries of what could be considered practice, it is still virtually impossible for men and women to communicate either easily or particularly successfully. To alleviate the problem somewhat, my mother and I have devised an all-purpose questionnaire, which can be used to help you discover—if not actually understand—what is going on in that male mind.

1. You haven't spoken to me in eight days. The reason you haven't spoken to me in eight days is that:
   a. You're mad at me.
   b. You're depressed.
   c. You have no idea.

2. If you are mad at me, you're mad at me because:
   a. I said I was going to Tulsa to see my sister for a few days.
   b. Your favorite socks faded in the wash because I insisted on using the environment-friendly detergent.
   c. You have no idea.

3. Last month, I didn't speak to you for nearly a week. This was because:
   a. You never noticed I wasn't speaking to you.
   b. You thought I must be getting my period.
   c. You knew I seemed a little distant, but you couldn't figure out why.

4. Now that you know I wasn't speaking to you, would you like to know why?
   a. I guess so.
   b. If you feel you have to tell me.
   c. Don't know.

5. The reason you get so upset when I go to visit my sister is that:
   a. You miss me.
   b. You worry about me.
   c. You're afraid my sister will tell me you put the moves on her the New Year's Eve you drank all that tequila and passed out in the bathtub.
   d. Don't know.

6. The reason you made such a big stink about one of your socks fading is:
   a. You really loved those socks and they can never be replaced.
   b. You're confusing me with your mother.
   c. Don't know.

7. Not long after the fight about your socks, you said that you wished I looked more like Julia Roberts. When I asked you what you meant by that you turned on the television. What you meant by that was that:
   a. You don't think Julia Roberts is the kind of woman who would fade one of your favorite socks.
   b. You wouldn't care if Julia Roberts shredded your favorite socks and served them to you for breakfast because you think she's so beautiful.

    c. Everything would be all right if I were someone else . . . someone like Julia Roberts.

    d. You have no idea what you meant by that.

8. The first thing you do when I say that we have to talk is turn on the television. Why do you do this?

    a. Because there's something on television that you really want to see.

    b. Because I'm not Julia Roberts.

    c. Don't have a clue.

9. I've been giving a lot of thought lately to moving in with my sister. What do you think of this idea?

    a. If that's what you want, you should do it.

    b. You don't have to.

    c. Don't know.

10. What do you mean "I don't have to"?

    a. I mean you don't have to.

    b. I mean I'd prefer it if you didn't.

    c. I mean I don't want you to leave.

    d. Don't know.

11. Every night you come home from work, you change into your old clothes, and you go out to the garage and work on the car. Whenever I want to do something, even if it's just talk, you say you can't because you're busy. Why do you do this?

    a. Because I'm eager to get the car fixed.

    b. Because I'm still getting over the death of the dog.

    c. No idea.

12. On the 14th of May, you and I went to a movie and then out to dinner. We had a good time. We laughed a lot and we talked so much that we closed the restaurant. You drove me home. "I'll call you Monday," you told me. On the 16th of June you called me. "Hi," you said. "This is

Jim. I've got tickets to a play on Saturday night. Are you free?" Why did it take you a month to call me?
a. Are you sure it was a month?
b. I was very busy.
c. I couldn't find my address book.
d. To be totally honest, I was dating someone else at the time and then I met you and we had so much fun, and I liked you so much, and it confused me and I didn't know what to do and I couldn't handle the situation so I decided just not to call you for a while.
e. Between Saturday night and Monday I got to thinking about your laugh and even though I had had a good time and enjoyed our conversation on true crime I just didn't feel like seeing you again right away.
f. I don't know.

13. Why are you calling me now?
a. Because I want to go out with you again.
b. Because the woman I was going out with on Saturday has stood me up.
c. Because the other woman I was seeing dumped me.
d. Because I was embarrassed that I never phoned as I promised, and so I wasn't going to, and then I was standing by the pasta in the supermarket and I suddenly remembered that joke you made about tortellini and I thought to myself, Don't be a dope. Call her and see if she'll give you another chance.
e. Don't know.

14. Sometimes you'll be in a bad mood for days. You'll schlump around the house, not speaking, not eating, just watching television shows you've seen before and yelling at the dog. But when I ask you what's wrong you say "Nothing." What, exactly, do you mean by "nothing"?
a. Nothing
b. Nothing that I want to talk to you about.

c. I mean that nothing's wrong—nothing that is related to you or that could actually be discussed in an open and adult manner—I'm just in one of those moods.

d. I don't know.

15. Why do you always leave the toilet seat up?

a. I don't.

b. I didn't think I did.

c. I don't know.

F

Fifteen Things About Men That Drive Women Crazy

1. *Self-centeredness.* Otherwise known as the genetic inability of the male to understand that the center of the universe is farther away from him than he thinks.

2. *Dysfunctional communication skills.* A man will talk to you for hours on end about the importance of the Gatling gun or how plastic bottles are made, but ask him about his feelings and he can't think of anything to say. "All right," he says. "Um." Unless, of course, he has feelings that have nothing to do with you, in which case you will spend years hearing how Lorna Watchceller broke his heart in 1985.

3. *Poor eyesight*, as illustrated by the fact that so many of them can't distinguish a woman from a girl.

4. *Competitiveness.* You start out playing a friendly game of Scrabble. First, he starts getting angry every time someone offers you some help. "Don't tell her about *axophyte*," he snarls. "It doesn't count if she can't get it on her own." Then he starts to sulk. "I'm not sulking," he says. "I just like to take my time." Not

long after that he accidentally knocks the board on the floor and declares the game a draw.

5. *Self-obsession*. Jack has a cold. Jack can barely get to the toilet without Jill's help, his cold is so bad. Jill spends several days nursing Jack, and then she, too, becomes ill. Only she doesn't have a cold, she has the flu. Her temperature is high, her eyes are glassy, bones and muscles she didn't know were in her body are screaming out with pain. "I have to go to bed myself," Jill tells Jack. "Gosh, I guess maybe you do," Jack gasps. "You look almost as bad as I feel."

6. *Priority distortion*, caused by the fact that for most purposes they are governed not by what lies beneath their skulls but by what lies beneath their flies.

7. *Domination complex*. You're painting the kitchen. You have painted the kitchen before. Your mother, a professional decorator, taught you everything she knew about painting kitchens, which was a considerable amount. Enter a man. Not your man, perhaps; perhaps not even a man you know. The phone man, maybe, or the guy who's fixing the video. Within five minutes, he will be standing at the foot of the ladder, telling you what you're doing wrong. "Did you clean it first?" he'll want to know. "You really should've primed it." No matter how many times you tell him that you are, in fact, an expert painter (a bit of information he could even deduce for himself) he won't listen. "You're putting it on too heavy," he'll say. "Try nice, even strokes . . ."

8. *Lack of intuition*. The reason men fall short on the intuition scales is because they tend to lack any real curiosity about other people or how they might be feeling. Some theoreticians claim this is because men are more involved with larger concepts (e.g., God, quantum mechanics, global destruction). My mother, however, maintains that it's because they only think about themselves.

9. *Self-dramatization*. Mary cooks a dinner for John's boss and a few important clients. It is a sit-down dinner for sixteen, perfect

from beginning to end. Mary does the shopping and preparation for the meal over a number of days, working it around her job, the children, taking the cat back and forth to the vet because of his ear, organizing the Opting for Otters campaign. When her best friend comes over on the afternoon of the dinner and notices the large quantities of shrimp and spinach in the fridge, Mary looks up from stuffing mushrooms and dancing with the toddler to say, "Oh, John's having some people over tonight." The following Sunday, John decides to make breakfast for the family. He begins at nine. By twelve he has everyone in the family following his orders, has used every bowl, pan and pot in the kitchen, and has produced one perfect pancake, which falls on the floor when he insists on flipping it over by throwing it in the air and catching it in the pan.

10. *Self-delusion*. The minute a man says, "I like women," or, "Actually, I'm a bit of a feminist myself," you can be pretty sure that the way he likes women are undressed and with their mouths filled with something other than words.

11. *Insensitivity*. An example of which is the fact that he can never figure out why you're so mad.

12. *The Pope Problem*. Like the pope, many men think that they are always right. Also like the pope, they are wrong about this, too.

13. *Absentmindedness*. Once again, theories differ, but it is generally assumed—at least by men—that the reason they have so much trouble keeping track of their keys, wallet, socks, the corkscrew, etc. is that they have their minds on larger issues (God, the origin of the universe, selling cereal). Althera Beryl Gray says that ten times out of ten the larger issue distracting men from remembering that it is possible to replace the toilet paper or even put the toilet seat down is when and what they're eating next and if they're likely to find someone to make wild, passionate love to them before they lose all their hair.

14. *Selective incompetency.* According to certain experts, the inability to work the washing machine, cook anything more complex than spaghetti, or tend to three young children for longer than an afternoon is not genetic, as many people like to think. It is simply because these are things they don't feel they should have to do, these are the things women are supposed to do so they can be free to think about larger issues like who's likely to win the World Series.

15. *The silence.*

Fooling Around

In the 1991 landmark case of *Smuthers* v. *N.Y. Tel.*, Jerry Smuthers, a thirty-six-year-old accountant, sued N.Y. Tel. for the breakup of his marriage.

"If they'd never brought in the itemized telephone bill, I would still be a happily married man today," said Jerry. "Instead I'm paying child support, alimony, and living over my mother's garage."

Kathleen Smuthers, testifying on behalf of N.Y. Tel, said that it was typical of her ex-husband to blame someone else for the failure of their marriage.

"The first thing Jerry said when I confronted him with the February phone bill and the one hundred and eighty calls to the same number in Vermont was, "Darling, it's not what you think." Kathleen, an attractive marketing executive in her early thirties, smiled in that ironic way that ex-wives often smile. "Until that moment I thought the phone company had made a mistake," she said. "I mean, why would anyone make nearly two hundred calls to the same number in a one-month period? I don't even talk to my best friend that much." But as soon as Jerry said, "Darling, it's not what you think," she knew he must be having an affair. She threw the cellular phone at him, narrowly missing blinding him in the left eye.

"Her behavior was completely irrational as usual," said Jerry. "I tried to explain that my relationship with Michelle was just one of those things. I met Michelle at a CPA convention in Denver. I'd given a lecture on hidden tax shelters and she came up to me later in the bar to tell me how fascinating she'd found it. I was flattered. Kathleen falls asleep whenever I start talking about work. She pretends to be interested, but you can see that her eyes are glazed over and she's really thinking about dinner or what the orthodontist said or something like that. In any event, I bought Michelle a drink and we sat around talking about tax shelters for a while. She laughed at my joke about the tax inspector and the showgirl, the one Kathleen never gets, and then she invited me up to her room to see the Personal Inventory Form she'd devised for her clients. I knew right then that she wanted me. I wasn't in love with her or anything—I love my wife and my children, that goes without saying—but she wanted me. What are you supposed to do when a woman wants you? When she practically throws herself into your arms? It wasn't as if I'd planned this. I didn't seduce Michelle. If anything, Michelle seduced me. I never wanted to hurt my wife. But do you think Kathleen understood that? No, Kathleen didn't understand that. 'This has nothing to do with you or our marriage,' I told her, but she wouldn't listen. Of course. You know what women are like. She kept waving the phone bill in my face and screaming, 'One hundred and eighty calls in one month and you can never even call me to tell me you're going to be late for dinner!' If that's not irrational, what is?"

Thought Questions:

1. Why does Jerry think his affair, unlike N.Y. Tel., had nothing to do with the breakup of his marriage?

2. If Jerry thought that it wasn't what Kathleen thought, what did Jerry think it was?

3. Why does Jerry think Kathleen behaved irrationally when she tried to brain him with his phone?

4. What is a man supposed to do when a woman who isn't his wife wants him?

5. Can you ever imagine a time when Michelle wouldn't laugh at Jerry's jokes anymore?

Fools for Love Anonymous

Fools for Love Anonymous, now a worldwide organization with a membership in the millions, began humbly enough in Miranda Hershey's living room on the Upper West Side of Manhattan in 1968. Miranda had just broken up with her latest boyfriend and she'd had enough.

"Forget drugs, alcohol, cigarettes, gambling, cookies, garlic-and-onion potato chips . . . as far as I was concerned, the most addictive substance in the universe was love," says Miranda. Miranda was one of those women who when watching *Moonstruck* for the fifteenth time still identified not with the mother or the mistress but with Cher. She still believed that Bob Dylan and Joan Baez would get back together. Now and then she still called the answering machine of her true but unrequited love, David Fumbleford, just to hear his voice.

Miranda admits, "One guy would be walking out the door with my blender and half my record collection, and I'd be looking around for the next. This one will be different, I'd tell myself. This one's going to be Mr. Right." She laughs, ironically. "I was a real sucker for romance," she confesses. "Candlelight . . . music . . . a walk beneath the stars . . ." She rolls her eyes. "They didn't even have to be big candles. There didn't have to be a lot of stars. Those tiny candles they have in churches and the Little Dipper were enough to set me off. And as for the music . . . I could fall in love to the bagpipe. I'd been known to cry over a Barry Manilow song. I was a hopeless case."

So, after years of unfulfilled relationships and sleepless, tear-soaked nights, Miranda Hershey decided to do something about it.

"I knew I wasn't the only one," she says. "Almost all my friends were in the same boat. You know how men are always going on quests to find the Holy Grail or the hidden city of the Incas or the Loch Ness monster or something like that? Well the only quest most women go on is to find Mr. Prince Charming. And they never find Mr. Prince Charming any more than these guys ever find Atlantis. If they're lucky, they find Mr. I Could Put Up With Him If I Really Had To. And so they do. They throw themselves into convincing themselves that this is the biggest romance since Romeo got Juliet killed—you know, squeezing into all this uncomfortable underwear, making sure his favorite cookies are in the house, listening to his stories about getting so drunk he fell asleep on the train and woke up in Philadelphia, picking up his allergy medicine, calling his penis Freddy—and then the next thing they know they're all alone again, and all they have to show for all that effort are a few wax stains on the tablecloth. So that's when the idea of FLA came to me. I thought if we banded together and gave each other support and were really honest with ourselves we'd finally be able to get free. If it works for drunks it can work for us, is what I thought."

Fools for Love Anonymous: The Ten-Step Program

1. I admit that I am a fool for love. All I have to hear is two bars of "Only You" and get a whiff of orange blossoms and I'm ready to bake my own bread and run out for the condoms.

2. I admit that I use love as an excuse for letting him keep his model airplanes in my fridge and never phoning when he's going to be six hours late for a date.

3. I realize that being a hopeless romantic is a form of insanity. If I could hear myself rationalizing the trip I took to Bolivia to get him out of jail I'd have myself put away.

4. I understand that I can reclaim control of my life. If this means that I can never listen to pop music, walk into a card shop, or eat in a dark restaurant again, then that's what I'll do.

5. I have made a cringe-making inventory of myself. I know that I would never have gotten involved in the mud wrestling if he hadn't said "I love you." I know that I would never have forgiven him the reverse phone calls from Beijing and the tap-dancing waitress from Houston if he hadn't said he couldn't live without me.

6. I have admitted to God, myself, all my friends, and several people I met on the bus that the fault is mine. Not only did I make myself a sitting target, but I loaded the gun, handed it to him, and showed him where to aim. If he hadn't been able to figure out how to pull the trigger, I would probably have done that for him too.

7. I will burn my copies of *Love Story*, *Wuthering Heights*, and *Cinderella*. I will only shop in stores that don't sell women's magazines, as women's magazines only encourage my dependency. I will melt all my candles and used the wax to block up the mouse holes. I will bury every tape, CD, and record I have that mentions the word *love*, which will probably leave me with one recording of the Red Army Choir and an album of Pete Seeger singing folk songs for children. I will move to a neighborhood that doesn't have a florist. I will sell my television to someone who can watch that commercial for instant coffee without bursting into tears.

8. I will give every video I have that has anything to do with love or romance—even my copy of *Moonstruck*—to the Salvation Army. This may mean that I have nothing left to watch but Bugs Bunny cartoons and samurai movies, but I will be a better person for it. I will certainly cry less in the long run.

9. Whenever I feel myself weakening and beginning to fantasize about falling in love again, I will write a list of all the things

I expected love to do for me (make me happy, make me feel good about myself, give my life meaning) and all the things it has done (make me poorer, give me gray hairs, ruin my diet, make me violent).

10. On Valentine's Day I will go on a retreat to the mountains with my women's group. We will drink still mineral water and reread *The Edible Woman* out loud. Anyone who mentions *champagne, flowers, cupid, hearts, love,* or *romance* will be fined. Any monies received will be donated to the local home for unwed mothers.

G

Girl Talk

Judy and I were sitting around the kitchen one evening, talking about the religious implications of the Big Bang Theory. I scooped up some guacamole with my corn chip. "So as you can see," I summed up, "it doesn't seem to me that the mere fact that we've discovered the edge of the universe either precludes or excludes the existence of God."

Judy sighed. "I had another big fight with Mike last night," she informed me. "I bet you can't guess what this one was about."

"I don't suppose it was about Shroedinger's cat?" I ventured.

"Go on," she said. "Take a guess." She laughed the laugh of a woman who has heard it all. As, indeed, she more or less had.

I shrugged. "It's not fair," I said. "You and Mike argue about everything. I've been around when you argued about how to boil water."

"You were there for the Bombay Duck argument, too," said Judy.

I winced at the memory. "He wouldn't believe me either."

"You or Madhur Jaffrey," said Judy. "You missed the best one though," she went on. "The one about the stain on the carpet?

73

It went on for hours. He kept pointing to this perfectly ordinary patch of carpeting and screaming, 'See the stain? Why can't you see the stain?' " She tossed back a couple of corn chips. "And then he has the nerve to say that I'm emotional and illogical."

"So what was this fight about? Whether or not the curtains had faded?"

Judy smirked. "You're going to love this," she said. She knocked back her beer. "We argued about whether or not women talk about men all the time. Can you imagine? He thinks I tell my friends everything about him, from how long it takes him to reach orgasm to what happened when he had that boil lanced."

"Seven minutes and he threw up."

"Anyway," Judy continued, "I told him. I said, 'Mike Mullholland, my friends and I have a lot more important things to talk about than you.' "

"And what did he say?"

"He said it's a well-known fact that if you get two women together, even if they're both world-class medievalists or prize-winning agronomists, within ten minutes they'll be talking about men." She laughed again. Hollowly this time. "There is no end to the male ego."

I opened two more beers. "Unlike the universe," I said.

Guy Things

Let's say that you, a woman, got a job in the local video store. It is your responsibility to check the tapes in and out. So what do you do? You check the tapes in and out in much the way that you would take in and give out the dry cleaning. It's a menial, less than exciting kind of job, but someone has to do it and you are that someone.

Let's say, however, that you are not a woman, you are a guy and you get a job in the local video store. Then what happens?

What happens is you get your ear pierced and start wearing a baseball cap backwards and an Iron Maiden T-shirt. Instead of being a salesclerk, you act as though you're a roadie for the Rolling Stones.

"Hang on a minute," you say. "It's not as though being a roadie for the Rolling Stones is any big deal. I mean, all you do is haul amps around and get yelled at for dropping the speakers."

That's the way a woman would see the job. But not a guy. A guy sees being a roadie as the next best thing to being able to play an electric guitar behind your back while so drunk you're not really sure what city you're in.

You frown, puzzled. "I'm not quite sure . . ."

Think about this. If a woman were a long-distance truck driver, that's what she'd be. She'd get into her truck and she'd drive it to its destination, and then she'd drive it back again. She'd be tired when she got home and she'd take a hot bath and fix herself a cup of strong coffee. Whenever anyone asked her what she did for a living she'd say, "I drive a truck." But not so a man. A man who drives a truck isn't just a truck driver, he's a warrior of the road. He gets a CB and a baseball cap and he puts a calendar featuring a half-naked woman at the back of the cab. He hangs out with other rough-and-tumble men of the road. They make movies and television commercials about him. He's a figure of romance and adventure, not a guy with a bad back and a dodgy stomach from eating at too many greasy spoons.

Your eyes narrow. "Oh, I get it. You're saying that men have the ability to turn even the smallest, most menial, most ordinary, or most insignificant activity into a guy thing."

Got it in one.

He Won't Talk to You When You're With Him, but He Will Once You've Left: The Phenomenon

"Bernie's driving me nuts," said Mandy. "Absolutely nuts."

We were sitting in the garden, sipping gin and tonic and talking about life as the sun went down over the skyline of Manhattan.

"What do you mean, Bernie's driving you nuts?" I asked. "You're divorced. He's remarried. You only speak to each other in monosyllables."

"You mean I only speak to him in monosyllables," said Mandy. She chewed reflectively on a sliver of lemon. "Nowadays he talks to me in novels."

I picked at something small that was trying to swim out of my drink. "Since when?" I asked.

"Since three months ago," said Mandy. "Everything was fine between us until then. We never spoke more than two words to each other, and those were rarely consecutive. If I'd moved to Buenos Aires he would never have known till I sent him a postcard."

I looked up. "Three months ago?" I tried to remember. "What happened three months ago?"

Mandy made a face. "Bernie married Yolanda, that's what happened."

"Oh, of course." I sighed in sympathy. "I'd forgotten about that."

"What a bummer," said Mandy. "I mean, really, Serena. For the first time in years everything was great with me and the Visitor from Another Planet. Total silence and lack of contact was a definite high point in my relationship with Bernie. I hadn't been so happy in years, and now it's all ruined. I must spend hours on the phone with him every week. He's calling me up to tell me his problems. For five years every time I asked what was wrong he said 'nothing' and now he can't shut up. Yolanda this . . . Yolanda that . . . I've heard about every fight, every slight, and every time she doesn't understand him. I know how much she spends on clothes, how long she spends in the bathroom . . . " She took a slug of gin. "Can you believe it? He even calls me at work. He even called me at four in the morning the other night, because she'd locked him out of the house."

"Why don't you just tell him to get lost?" I asked. "Why don't you just say, 'Bernie, you unmade your bed, now you can sleep in it.' "

Mandy swirled the ice in her glass. "I guess I'm just a very kind, generous, and understanding person," she said.

I swirled the ice in my glass. "And it makes you happy to know how unhappy he is."

Mandy smiled. "That too," she said.

His Wife Doesn't Understand Him, But Does He Understand Her?

A Quiz for Guys

Rare as the Ryukyu rabbit is the woman who has never had a man look soulfully into her eyes, sigh sadly, and say, "My wife doesn't understand me."

For a reason men have difficulty appreciating, the typical female response to this statement often falls short of a fulsome lament. Even the most kindly and sympathetic woman has been known to choke back a smirk and a giggle before saying, "No? Really? You poor thing," while the more jaded and embittered have a tendency to spit their Diet Coke across the table.

"What is it with you women?" ask the men. "Have you all become feminist manhaters? We know it's a bit of a cliché about a guy's wife not understanding him, but just because it's a cliché doesn't mean it's not true."

But women, of course, don't laugh because they don't think it's true that men's wives don't understand them. No one understands them. What women find amusing about the statement "My wife doesn't understand me" is the implication that he does understand her.

At this point in the conversation the men are darting little glances at one another and trying not to smirk themselves. Is there some suspicion that they don't understand women? Aren't their mothers women? Their sisters? Their lovers and wives? Their cleaning ladies? Haven't they lived with women all of their lives? Haven't they read *Playboy*? Haven't they heard of *Lady Chatterley's Lover*? Haven't they attended stag nights? Haven't they spent some of the best years of their lives watching beer ads and car commercials? One or two of them may even have purchased a box of tampons in his day. When you come right down to it, there can't really be very much about women that men don't know. Right?

Here's a little quiz for your significant or insignificant other, to see just how well he does know women.

A. *Multiple Choice*

Select the most appropriate answer based on what you know of your woman and/or women in general.

1. You have been seeing K for several years. It is an up-and-down relationship, as these things sometimes are, but fundamentally secure. You certainly feel secure. Periodically, K makes the sounds of a woman who would like to settle down and start tinkering with her biological clock, but you, though you know in your heart that when you do settle down it will be with K, haven't felt ready for so big a step yet. Also periodically, K and you have some dispute over money, your work and social obligations, the Green Bay Packers, or your feelings about her best friend that lead her to scream, "I never want to see you again as long as I live!" One of these lows in your relationship with K occurs after her sister's wedding. Not only did you, under the influence of a little too much cheap scotch, get a bit chummy with one of the bridesmaids, but when K caught the bouquet you kicked it out of her hands. As a result, K stops speaking to you well before the shrimp cocktail and—something she has never done before—leaves you to make your own way home. Why is K so angry?
   a. Because you have once more shown yourself to be insensitive to her feelings, thinking you could get away with behaving like a wild squirrel brought indoors because you'd had too much to drink.
   b. You have no idea. It's not as though this kind of thing hasn't happened before.
   c. Weddings make women hyperemotional. Thus, although you can see that K has a right to be annoyed—you shouldn't have danced so close to whateverhername-

79

was, and you definitely shouldn't have lobbed the bridal bouquet into the punch—you also know that had you been at something less emotionally charged she wouldn't have stabbed you with the pin from her corsage or thrown your car keys into the fountain.

2. When you call K at work the next day to get things back to normal, she refuses to speak to you. This is not untypical. Like most women, K is stubborn and moody, and, besides, she likes to make you suffer. You call her at home that night, and you get the answering machine. You get the answering machine at seven o'clock the next morning and at every hour between seven that night and two-forty-five the next day as well. This is not untypical, either. God only knows what women did before some man, making life easier for them as usual, invented the answering machine, but now that they have it they use it shamelessly. The next step is for you to turn up at her door, looking both apologetic and subdued, and demanding she stop being childish and sit down and talk. You turn up. No one answers. You run around the corner and use the pay phone. You get the answering machine. You hang up and call again. You get the answering machine again. "I know you're there!" you bellow to the amusement of the woman who is waiting behind you. "Pick up the damn phone!" As the woman prepares to take your place at the phone, she touches your arm. "Try writing a letter," she suggests. "Tell her how you really feel." You try writing a letter. In it you tell K how you really feel. You tell her how you always assumed that some-day she and you would be starting off the disco at your own wedding to a passionate rendition of "I Believe in Love." You tell her of the deep respect and affection in which you hold her. You tell her how empty your life would be without her. The next day on your way to work, you slip the letter under K's door. When you get home that night, the telephone is ringing. It is K. She

a. is crying. She begs you to come right over.

b. is crying too much for you to understand what she's saying. You go right over.

c. wants to know why it took you so long to tell her how you feel.

3. As it turns out, the only reason K wanted you to come over was so she could give you back everything you ever gave her (the slow cooker, the electric vegetable chopper, the black lace bustiere, the blouse whose color made her look like she had jaundice and which would have fit the saleswoman who sold it to you a lot better than it ever fit K). It seems that this time when K said, "I never want to speak to you again as long as I live!" she actually meant it. How were you supposed to know that this time was different from all those other times?

a. If you'd been paying attention during the last few months, you would have seen the signs.

b. You should have realized what time of month it was.

c. There's no way you could have known.

4. The reason it took you so long to tell K how you really felt about her was because you assumed that she already knew. How could she not have known? You took her fishing with you, didn't you? You let her drive your car. You have a toothbrush and a drawer full of socks and underwear at her place. You introduced her to your best friend. How could she not have known?

a. She knew. But women are emotionally needy and constantly want to be reassured.

b. She didn't want to know.

c. Maybe women aren't as intuitive as you've always been told.

d. She didn't know because the occasional positive comment on her pasta sauce or how she looks in those black stretch jeans cannot be construed as a wild and unbridled declaration of love. Not even by you.

5. Some old friends of your wife's, passing through town on their way somewhere else, stop by for a visit. Their names are Jack and Janet. Jack is not only astoundingly handsome for an award-winning photojournalist, but as the evening progresses you begin to get the feeling that he knows your wife a lot better than you thought at first—perhaps even biblically. The two of them keep laughing over jokes no one else understands. They smile at each other a lot and begin almost every sentence with "Remember that time . . ." or "Do you still have . . ." Janet, who has breasts like melons (were melons soft and warm and covered in red silk shirts only buttoned two-thirds of the way), seems more interested in the cat than in how often your wife and her husband brush against each other. By the time you and your wife turn in for the night, you are less than happy. You slam into the bedroom. You throw yourself under the quilt. Your wife, on some kind of hormonal high, pays not the tiniest bit of attention. "Don't you think Jack's wonderful, darling?" she asks with a seductive sigh as she slips between the sheets. You behave like a nuclear bomb that has just had its detonator button pushed. You begin by hissing, so your guests won't hear you, but you end up shouting loudly enough to wake the people next door. You accuse your wife of inviting Jack to your home solely to humiliate you. You accuse her of doing more in the kitchen with him than making the coffee. You say that it wouldn't surprise you if she'd been secretly having an affair with Jack all the time you and she have been married. Your wife

   a. tells you to stop being such a complete jerk. "Don't think you can fool me," she says. "I know what you're up to. You think if you accuse me of flirting with Jack, I won't say anything about the way you kept staring at Janet's breasts all night."

b. either bursts into tears or refuses to speak to you for the next two days. This is due to guilt.

c. cries, "Darling, I do believe you're jealous!" She really loves it when you're jealous.

6. Tonight's the night. You and your new love have finally agreed to do the deed. You're so excited and so nervous (Will you get it up? Will it stay up? For how long?) that it isn't until you are racing from the train that you remember the talk the two of you had about safe sex. You nip into the drugstore at the station and grab the first pack of condoms you see, only looking closely enough to make sure it doesn't say SMALL. You take a cab to the home of your paramour. She opens the door and you fall into each other's arms. So great is your mutual lust and desire that you are half-undressed before you hit the bedroom. Showing considerable physical dexterity, you manage to open the pack and roll on the condom while continuing to shower her with passionate kisses. "Are you ready, darling?" you whisper huskily. She glances at your throbbing member. She can't speak, because she's so overcome with lust, but if she could she would

a. say, "Hurry, my darling . . . take me now . . ."

b. cry out your name again and again.

c. start to laugh uncontrollably. She would point to your penis in its red condom. "My God!" she would shriek. "It looks like a hot dog!"

7. It's been a long, hard week. If you were a soft-drink dispenser instead of a sales director, you'd be empty, dented, and your change machine wouldn't be working. All you want to do is kick off your shoes, pour yourself a beer, and collapse on the sofa for the next two days. You come home from work as usual and enter your home. Unlike as usual, there is no smell of something charring in the kitchen, no sound of the smoke alarm going off. "Darling!" you call. "Darling, I'm home!" The dog comes

rushing out to greet you, hurling himself against your legs, but there is no answering, "Here I am, sweetheart! How was your day?" From experience, you know that there are two possible places where your cohabitor might be if she isn't busy cremating your dinner. 1. She is out spending your money. 2. She is sitting in the living room with her arms folded across her lap, mad at you. You put your things on the table in the hall and poke your head into the living room in a wary manner. There she is, pretending, in fact, to be reading the evening paper. You smile. "Hi," you say. She turns a page. You sigh. You are in no condition to play the What Have I Done Now? Game. "Okay," you say. "I give up. Now what have I done?" She doesn't look at you as she says, "You know." "No I don't," you say. "What is it?" She turns another page. "Think about it," she says. "You know." Do you know?

   a. You could make a good guess.
   b. It's that time of month.
   c. No.

8. Chances are, the reason she is so angry is that:
   a. Her best friend's husband gave her best friend something your wife wishes you'd given her.
   b. It's that time of month.
   c. For the thirteenth time in thirteen years, you've forgotten either her birthday or your anniversary.
   d. She found out.

9. You and your significant other are invited to a fancy cocktail party that has to do with your work (like your S.O., you are very successful at what you do). The other men have all brought their significant others, too, and like yours they hover to one side, clutching their wineglasses, smiling pleasantly, and listening attentively. By anybody's standards, it is a good evening. The wine is drinkable, the food is both edible and plentiful, and you got to talk to a

lot of like-minded professionals in a relaxed social atmosphere. "Well," you say as you get into the car beside your significant other, "that was all right, wasn't it?" In answer, she starts the car so quickly that your head hits the windshield. "The next time you have a work party, you can go on your own!" she screams. "Either that or I'm bringing an Uzi with me and I'm mowing down every man in the place!" Why is your beloved so upset?

a. As is usual at functions of this kind, significant others were encouraged only to speak to each other, and only then if they weren't interfering with another, more important conversation. In the course of three hours, therefore, your S.O. was asked only three questions: 1. Where's the toilet? 2. Where did you get the shrimp? 3. And how many children do you have?

b. It's that time of month.

c. The party made her go off her diet.

10. Much to everyone's amazement, you didn't forget your anniversary this year. You sent your wife a card and flowers, and then you took her out for a romantic champagne dinner. As she was sipping her double espresso, you tenderly whispered, "Let's go home, darling. I have a very special surprise for you." When you got home, you presented her with a large silver box tied with a red bow. "What is it?" she cried excitedly. "That tweed suit I pointed out in the mall last week? That IBM software I've had my heart set on? Tickets for a vacation in Santa Fe?" The answer is: None of the Above. The silver box contained a black-and-red silk-and-lace bustiere, complete with black lace garter belt and black net stockings. The reason you chose this as the perfect present for the mother of your children was that:

a. It was so sexy you practically passed out when the salesperson was showing it to you.

b. You found it on the bus.

c. You thought she'd appreciate the joke.

11. Instead of ripping off her clothes, pulling on the bustiere and the stockings, putting the complimentary copy of "The Stripper" that came with the lingerie on the stereo, and treating you to a private anniversary show, your life's partner let out a horrified, "What the hell is that?" and jumped back as though there were a dead rabbit in the box. The reason she reacted like this is that:

   a. She thinks that black lace bustieres, garter belts, and net stockings, though they may appeal to the sexual fantasies of the adolescent male, are about as titillating as having some guy expose himself to her on the subway.

   b. Her convent-school background prevents her from showing her true feelings.

   c. She was teasing you.

12. Even though you finally managed to remember your anniversary, you wife was still angry. She was angry because

   a. You have no idea why she was angry.

   b. It was that time of month.

   c. You wouldn't have remembered if she hadn't reminded you.

13. You come home from work one evening to hear the sixty-cycle hum of female conversation coming from the kitchen. You smell red wine and double-cheese pizza with peppers and mushrooms as well. Hungry and not averse to a glass of Chianti, you head toward the kitchen. As soon as you enter an unearthly hush falls over the room and all eyes turn toward you. The reason your cohabitor and her friends all shut up and look at you like that when you appear is that:

   a. They were talking about you.

   b. They were talking about men or blood.

c. You've interrupted them.

d. They know that unless you have work to do their conversation is all over.

14. Gala Dali, wife of the painter Salvador, was once quoted as saying that the reason she never had any children was that she had Dali. What did she mean by this?

a. That she was so in love with him she couldn't bear the thought of anyone else distracting her attention.

b. She couldn't have children, but she didn't like to come out and say it in case people thought it was his fault.

c. That she didn't have children because she had Dali.

15. It is Valentine's Day. What would your significant other most like as a token of your great affection?

a. A ferret of some size, shape, or description (she's mad about ferrets).

b. You have no idea, so you get her chocolates.

c. A big box of chocolates.

16. You wake up on Friday morning with a bit of a headache and the general feeling that it would be a good day for just mooching around the house. You call in sick. Your wife would also like to just mooch around the house today, but she has the kind of day lined up that would make the Terminator look lazy. Off she goes to raise her blood pressure and aggravate her ulcer, while you stay home and mooch. You have just finished the pizza you ordered and are putting a new video into the machine when your wife finally staggers into the hall. She stands framed in the doorway for a second, just gazing at you. She glances at the empty pizza box. She takes in the pile of videos. "Hi, sweetheart," you say. "How was your day?" Without answering—unless an undignified and rather bovine-sounding snort could be considered an answer—she marches into the bedroom, slamming the door behind her with such force that your beer can shakes. What has prompted this behavior?

a. Damned if you know.

b. It must be that time of the month.

c. She's tired.

d. She's tired, she's had a hard day, the breakfast dishes are still in the sink, and you didn't wait let alone fix supper for her.

17. You and your cohabitor are watching television one night when a new car advertisement comes on. In it a couple are setting off to visit friends they haven't visited before. The husband is behind the wheel. The wife, equipped with the directions sent them by their friends and a map, tries to act as navigator, but her husband won't listen to her advice. "Of course I know what I'm doing," he keeps saying. "Of course this is the right way." When the couple begin their journey, it is daylight and the car is sparkling clean. By the time they find themselves perched on top of a cliff in the middle of nowhere it is dark and the car looks like it's been on a rather arduous safari in the rainy season. What does your cohabitor think of this advertisement?

a. She doesn't say so in so many words, but you're pretty sure that it reminds her of you.

b. It doesn't occur to you to wonder.

c. She makes no comment, but you're pretty sure she finds it as baffling as you do.

18. You and your partner are having problems and agree to separate. Because neither of you wants to separate permanently, however, you agree to seek professional help. The counselor says that the two of you should see as much of each other as you want, but that under no circumstances are you to sleep together. The counselor advises you against physical intimacy because:

a. Women take sex so seriously.

b. Knowing how women are, the counselor is afraid your

partner might misunderstand your motives for sleeping with her and complicate the situation.

c. Men think women take sex so seriously.

19. Many women become upset, not to say incensed, when referred to as "girls." "Just who do you think you're calling a girl, buster?" they demand right before they deck you with a right hook or dump their drink in your lap. Women who react like this to such an innocent word do so because:

a. They think you're being patronizing even if you don't.

b. They're flirting with you.

c. They're feminists with bad attitudes.

20. One night while getting ready for bed, your cohabitor says to you, "Darling, do you think I'm putting on weight?" She asks you this because:

a. She's mad about something you don't know about and she's trying to pick a fight.

b. She wants to know if she's putting on weight.

c. She doesn't want to know if she's putting on weight.

d. She'd like a little reassurance that you find her attractive.

21. You and the light of your life go to a function at the school together. It is a boring function as these things go (making it a minus ten on a scale of one to ten), but you and your life's light make a point to support the school, and you are the secretary of the PTA, a role you take quite seriously. In any event, the night grows damp and chilly and as soon as the drum solos and recitations are through, your beloved wants to leave. You say, "Darling, we can't go now. We have to stay to talk to the staff and the principal." She says, "Oh no we don't. I have to get up at six tomorrow morning, and I want to leave now." "Be reasonable," you plead—though as she has never been known to be reasonable before why she should start now is open to debate. She storms off, the car keys jangling

from her hands. Just as it begins to rain, you leave too. You take two buses and a train home. When you get home you see, through the sitting-room window, the baby sitter, curled up on the couch, eating chips and watching television. With the same sinking feeling Montezuma had when he saw Cortez approaching Mexico City, you know that your housewife is not in the house, but sitting in the car around the corner from the school—in the dark, and the rain, and the dead of night. Why didn't she go home and leave you, like she said she was going to do?

a. Because she is not the kind of person to make another person take two buses and a subway home, even if this same person once left her at the mall because she couldn't make up her mind between the blue bathing suit and the orange and purple.

b. She probably couldn't get the car started.

c. She's playing with your head.

22. Your significant other, a scientist and writer of some repute, needs to purchase a new computer. This will be her third. You offer to go along with her to look at computers because, although you will be as much use to her as you were when your children were born (you fainted), you like to play Kung Fu Warrior while she talks megabytes and RAMs with the salesman. She says you can come for the ride, but you have to sit in the car while she goes into the store. The reason she doesn't want you with her is that:

a. She's been reading Marilyn French again.

b. She doesn't want to drive with you in the car because she doesn't want you to yell at her for riding the clutch.

c. If you go into Computerland with her the salesman will ignore her and talk to you.

23. You come home from work to find your significant other marching around the kitchen like a Nazi marching

around Poland. "Can you believe it?" she wants to know. "I bought an answering machine today and when I got it home I found out that it doesn't work!" She throws something into the oven and slams the door. "Now I have to go back tomorrow." You say:

a. "I'd be happy to take it back for you, dear, but you know I'm hopeless with anything with a plug. I'd probably come back with a Fax machine."

b. "You think that's something? Wait till you hear about my day."

c. "Are you sure you set it up right?"

24. After you say, "Are you sure you set it up right, dear?" your significant other stares at you in silence for just about a nanosecond. And then she throws the kettle at your head and storms from the room. She behaves in this childish and emotional way because:

a. She hates to be reminded that she's hopeless when it comes to electrical equipment.

b. It's that time of the month.

c. A woman who makes her own computer programs and her own ravioli can be assumed to be capable of setting up a computer without male assistance.

25. Your significant other joins you and several of your friends from the office for a night on the town. Originally, there were going to be other women along, so yours would have someone to discuss diets with, but none of them could make it. Your significant other suddenly raps on the table with her teaspoon as dessert is being served. "Okay, guys," she says loudly. "I've spent the better part of four hours listening to you drone on about your problems at work and what the chances are that your team's going to get into the Series. Now we're going to talk about me for a while." Why does she do this?

a. She is bored rigid.

b. PMS.

c. She drank too much.

26. You and your lady love don't exactly have a fight, but there is a bit of a disagreement about whether or not you should go to San Francisco by yourself. For several days after your return you call her but get the answering machine. The first day you leave a message. She doesn't call back. The second day you leave a message. She doesn't call back. By the fourth day even you begin to wonder if she's out of town or avoiding your calls. You don't leave a message on the fifth day. On the sixth day you call when she would least expect it—at a time when you are normally sound asleep—and she picks up on the second ring. "Hi, hon," she says. "How was your trip?" She is chatty, bubbly, and sweet as cherry cola. What does this mean?

   a. There was something wrong with her answering machine.

   b. She has never properly mastered her answering machine.

   c. She's still mad about San Francisco.

   d. She'd like to remove your liver with a grapefruit spoon.

B. *Yes/No/Don't Know.*

For each of the following statements, indicate whether you agree, don't agree, or have no idea.

1. Women who describe themselves as feminists don't like men.

2. Women talk more about men than men talk about women.

3. Unlike men, who are logical and rational, women are victims of their body chemistry.

4. A man can work beside another man for twenty years,

and the most he'll know about the other man is what team he supports, what party he votes for, what beer he drinks, where he went to school, the names of his wife and children, and whether or not he likes dogs. Let the wives of these men spend an elevator ride from the ground floor to the twenty-third together, however, and by the time they disembark they will each know how much the other's husband makes, what kind of food he likes, what his temperament and sense of humor are like, whether he's impotent, ejaculates prematurely or has boils, which side of the bed he sleeps on, whether they're having marital problems or if he's worried about his job, and what their last argument was about.

5. When your significant other complains that you never talk to her she doesn't really mean that you never talk to her. What she means is that you never talk to her about things like vaginal yeast infections the way her girlfriends do.

6. Ever since you saw *When Harry Met Sally* it's occurred to you that there must have been times in your life when the woman you thought you were thrilling was actually composing a shopping list and waiting to go to sleep.

7. The reason you never realized before that while you thought your partner in passion was whimpering with ecstasy when in reality she was deciding between chicken and fish sticks is because women are so innately deceitful.

8. Men gossip just as much, if not more, than women do.

9. Not through choice but because your lover keeps renting it out of the video store, you have seen *Thelma and Louise* at least half a dozen times. You still have no idea why they get so mad at that truck driver.

10. Men don't make passes at girls who wear glasses because

girls who wear glasses just aren't as attractive as girls who don't. (In the interests of any incipient feminists out there, they don't make passes at women who wear glasses either.)

11. Every now and then—usually at a public gathering like a party when spirits are high and guards are down—you catch your significant other's best friend giving you a certain look. It is a look that is both curious and intimate. You, of course, would never take advantage of this situation, but it's pretty obvious that she's interested in you in a carnal way.

12. Women who are quiet and feminine and interested in being wed do like men.

13. Your girlfriend gives you the cold shoulder all night, sitting as far away as she can, answering your questions with monosyllables, smiling woodenly at your amusing anecdotes. You finally notice this behavior when she comes to bed in her pajamas with the feet in them and the terrycloth robe. You ask her what's wrong. She says, "You know." You do know.

14. She doesn't really think you know, she's just saying that to wind you up.

15. It's true that if bearing children were the responsibility of men there would be no problem with overpopulation.

16. The fact that you often don't know why the woman in your life is angry with you is not because you are evasive and refuse to confront issues and emotions (as has sometimes been suggested), but because she is often angry over some imaginary slight.

17. Women aren't congenitally more jealous than men are.

18. You know that your girlfriend is seeing someone else. You

know this because you have been reading her diary. When you confront her with your knowledge she bursts into tears. Eventually, she admits that she was attracted to this other man, but she says she hasn't slept with him. You believe her because of a sentence in her diary. That sentence is: I refuse to spend the night with P in a cheap motel.

19. Women have no more of a talent for making a big deal out of absolutely nothing than men do.

Scoring

In section A, score yourself as follows: Subtract 1 point for every B answer and add 3 points for every D answer. In the even-numbered questions, give yourself 1 point for every A answer and 2 points for every C. In the odd-numbered questions, give yourself 2 points for every A answer and 1 point for every C.

In Section B, score yourself as follows:

1. Women who describe themselves as feminists tend, in fact, to have a low jerk-tolerance level. Give yourself −1 point for a Yes; 2 points for a No; and −1 for a Don't Know.

2. In reality, men talk as much about women as women talk about men. The difference lies not in quantity but in quality. Talking about breasts is not the same as talking seriously about people, their character, problems, and instincts. Give yourself 1 point for a Yes; −1 for a No; and 1 for a Don't Know.

3. And men are under penis control. −2 for a Yes; 2 for No; 0 for a Don't Know.

4. Because men, like children under three, are egocentric; it never occurs to them to wonder about those outside of themselves. 1 for a Yes; −1 for a No; 0 for a Don't Know.

5. No, she means you never talk to her. −2 for a Yes; 2 for a No; 1 for a Don't Know.

6. It took you a while. Give yourself 1 for a Yes; −2 for a No; 0 for a Don't Know.

7. It's more likely because men are so vain. −2 for a Yes; 2 for a No; 1 for a Don't Know.

8. They certainly don't gossip less. 2 for a Yes; −1 for a No; 1 for a Don't Know.

9. If you answered Yes it's lucky you're not a truck driver since you're clearly asleep at the wheel. −2 for a Yes; 1 for a No; 0 for a Don't Know.

10. No, it's because men think glasses are a sign of intelligence. −1 for a Yes; 1 for a No; 2 for a Don't Know.

11. Actually what that look means is "What does Alice see in him?" −2 for a Yes; 2 for a No; 1 for a Don't Know.

12. This is a pretty serious misconception. −2 for a Yes; 2 for a No; 1 for a Don't Know.

13. Actually, you probably don't know. Though you probably should. 2 for a Yes; 1 for a No; 2 for a Don't Know.

14. She knows that you should know. 2 for a Yes; 2 for a No; 2 for a Don't Know.

15. It is true. 1 for a Yes; −1 for a No; 0 for a Don't Know.

16. It's probably because you're evasive and refuse to confront issues. 0 for a Yes; 2 for a No; 1 for a Don't Know.

17. Not by a long shot, sunshine. 2 for a Yes; −2 for a No; 0 for a Don't Know.

18. You shouldn't read her diary, of course, but if you do you should at least hone your analytical skills a little more. What's the use of breaching a moral trust like that if the

information you gather is useless to you? It's like stealing a diamond worth millions and then keeping it in the refrigerator because you don't know what to do with it. The fact that she refuses to spend the night in a cheap motel with P doesn't mean she didn't spend a torrid afternoon there, it just means that the room is small or the mattress is too uncomfortable if you're actually planning to sleep on it. −2 for a Yes; 2 for a No; 1 for a Don't Know.

19. You do remember WWI, don't you? −3 for a Yes; 2 for a No; −2 for a Don't Know.

39 points and below: It would be impossible to know less about women without coming from another planet. Since this is unlikely to be your excuse, it would be interesting to know what your excuse is.

40–50 points: You wouldn't want to find yourself at Germaine Greer's birthday party, that's for sure, but you are at least making an effort.

51–76 points: You might actually enjoy Germaine's birthday party—and escape with your life.

77–88 points: You're either one of the most sensitive, understanding and intelligent men in the world, kidding yourself, or lying.

Hope Against Hope

A Case Study

My mother and I both believe that it is possible to gain from the experience of others. "You don't have to hang from a gibbet in Tucson in the summer to know that it's something you'd rather not do," my mother is fond of saying. My mother and I also believe that the importance of stomping hope into the ground when you're trying either to get out or stay out of a failed relationship can't be overemphasized. "Keeping even the smallest, most infinitesimal sliver of hope alive is like continually playing Russian roulette," says my mother. "Sooner or later you're going to blow your brains out." So here is a true story from my files that you can profit from, thus saving yourself the bother of having to go through this ordeal yourself.

BEATRICE: [entering the room like a hurricane entering Florida] This is it, Dr. Gray! I've made up my mind. As soon as I leave here, I'm calling Marshall and I'm telling him that we're through. Finished. Finito. Kaput. [noticing the expression on his face] You look skeptical, Dr. Gray.

S.G.: Not skeptical, Beatrice. Concerned. Let's not forget that you have broken up with Marshall before.

BEATRICE: That was different.

S.G.: [gently] Um, Beatrice, just how many times have you broken up with Marshall in the past?

BEATRICE: How many? [starts counting on her fingers] Let's see. . . . There was the summer after we met. . . . There was the following Halloween . . . then that Christmas and on New Year's Eve . . . Easter . . . my birthday . . . June . . . November . . . Christmas and New Year's. . . . Thirty-one, not including the time on the ferry.

S.G.: Thirty-one, not including the time on the ferry. . . .

BEATRICE: I know what you're thinking, Dr. Gray. You're thinking that this time is going to be like all the rest, but you're wrong. This time really is different. This time I mean it.

S.G.: This time you mean it.

BEATRICE: That's right, Dr. Gray. Marshall Oppoodle, doctor of dental surgery, has stood me up for the last time.

S.G.: It wasn't your birthday again, was it?

BEATRICE: No. My birthday was when I waited at the airport for him for sixteen hours.

S.G.: His birthday?

BEATRICE: [shaking her head] No, his birthday was when I waited in that hotel in Maine for three days.

S.G.: Your anniversary?

BEATRICE: [nodding] And he didn't even send me flowers this year. Last year he sent me a dozen red roses, but this year he didn't send me so much as a daisy. He said he'd be there at seven, right after he finished Mrs. Sutter's crowns. I made all his favorite things. Duckling in cherry sauce. Wild rice. Sautéed truffles. Homemade ice cream. . . .

S.G.: Isn't that the same meal you made for your first, second, third, and fourth anniversaries?

BEATRICE: Five years, can you believe it?

S.G.: I can believe it. What I can't believe is that in five years he's never tasted this duck or this ice cream.

BEATRICE: Five years, and the only time he's ever turned up when he said he would was the summer his wife went to Alaska because there weren't any phones where she was staying. I couldn't even count on him when she was in the hospital that time because he felt too guilty.

S.G.: How long did you wait last night?

BEATRICE: [examining her nails evasively] I don't really know.

S.G.: You don't know? You threw out your watch?

BEATRICE: [hesitantly] Well, I called the police at about nine, just to make sure there hadn't been any accidents between Marshall's house and my—

S.G.: Beatrice—how many times—

BEATRICE: But it could happen, Dr. Gray. People are always dying tragically in car crashes. Just because Marshall was never killed in one before—

S.G.   Beatrice—

BEATRICE: Or he could have broken down. I'm always after him to get a cellular phone, you know, so he could tell me if he had a flat or got lost or there was some freak thunderstorm on the way from Scarsdale. . . .

S.G.:   So what did you do after you called the police?

BEATRICE: I called the hospitals.

S.G.:   The hospitals? What for?

BEATRICE: I thought he might have had a heart attack or something while he was walking to his car. Or maybe he stopped at a McDonald's, you know, to call me to tell me he was going to be late because he had a flat, and he was hit by a car in the parking lot.

S.G.:   You thought Marshall Oppoodle was hit by a car in the parking lot of a McDonald's on the way to Brooklyn?

BEATRICE: That same thing happened just last week. I read about it in the paper.

S.G.:   Then what did you do?

BEATRICE: I called his office, just in case there'd been some problem with Mrs. Sutter and he was running late? But all I got was the answering machine.

S.G.:   And then?

BEATRICE: And then it suddenly hit me. Maybe the cat had knocked my phone off the hook or something, so I went and checked that.

S.G.:   Had the cat knocked the phone off the hook?

BEATRICE: No, and there wasn't anything wrong with the line. I went to the corner and called myself and it was just fine.

S.G.:   Front doorbell working?

BEATRICE: Uh huh.

S.G.:   The phone was working, the bell was working. . . . What did you do next?

100

BEATRICE: I was going to open the champagne, but then I thought that if he did come he wouldn't be too happy if I'd finished all the champagne by myself, he hates it when I'm drunk, so I made some coffee and—

S.G.: You didn't eat?

BEATRICE: Well I didn't want to start without him—and, anyway, I don't really like duck.

S.G.: Of course not. So you made yourself some coffee . . .

BEATRICE: By then the candles had burned down, so I was sitting there in the dark, wondering if I should put the oven on again, you know, so if he did show up everything wouldn't be cold, or if I should put the duck in the refrigerator because I wasn't sure if it was like turkey and you could get salmonella from it if you left it sitting around for a while, and that was when I got to thinking.

S.G.: And what did you think?

BEATRICE: It suddenly occurred to me that Marshall is probably never going to leave his wife.

S.G.: Probably?

BEATRICE: [her hand freezing in the act of removing a pack of tissues from her bag] You mean you think he might? You think it'd be a mistake to give up so soon?

S.G.: No, I—

BEATRICE: Well, of course I didn't mean to say I thought he'd never leave her. He'll leave her someday, I'm sure of that. He's so unhappy. . . . And it isn't easy for him to leave, of course. I mean, there's the kids, and the apartment, and the house in the country, and his practice. People are funny about divorced dentists. And there's no telling what she might do, she's so unstable. He will leave her, I'm sure he'll leave her, I just meant that he's proba-

101

bly not going to leave her really soon, you know, like in the next—

S.G.: Beatrice, I—

BEATRICE: —few months or anything like that, even though she makes him so miserable. She really doesn't understand him, Dr. Gray, it just about breaks my heart. Did I tell you what she did last week?

S.G.: I'm sure you—

BEATRICE: She told him she hated his guitar playing. Can you imagine? She must know how impor-

S.G.: Beatrice, you really have to—

BEATRICE: Think about this seriously, I know, Dr. Gray. You're right. I got myself into a state last night, but I shouldn't be too hasty. I mean, what if I stop seeing Marshall and then he does leave her? What then? He'll think that I'm unreliable. My love will have been tested and found wanting. I mean, if I do love him—and you know I love him— then it's my duty to stick by him, isn't it? I mean, what kind of love is it if it can't withstand a little—

S.G.: [slightly raising my voice above the acceptable professional level] Beatrice, you have to get a grip on yourself. I thought you just told me that you'd realized last night that Marshall would never leave his wife.

BEATRICE: Oh my gosh, Dr. Gray, didn't I ever tell you what happened to my cousin's sister's best friend, Georgina? About how she had this affair with a married man, and finally after six or seven years she broke it off and then, five years later, just as she was about to leave for the airport to take a new job in Chicago, she got this phone call from him. He'd left his wife and he was ready to marry Georgina. And she married him and they

102

lived happily ever after. So you see, the same thing could happen to me.

S.G.:　　It could never happen to you, Beatrice. Remember when you were offered that promotion and you wouldn't take it because it meant moving to Pittsburgh?

BEATRICE:　I don't think Chicago's the important part of the story, Dr. Gray. It could still happen to me.

S.G.:　　And pigs might fly.

BEATRICE:　Are you saying it's hopeless?

S.G.:　　Yes, Beatrice, yes I am.

BEATRICE:　Completely hopeless?

S.G.:　　Yes, Beatrice, completely hopeless.

BEATRICE:　But how can you be so sure?

Thought Questions:

1. Why does Beatrice think that Marshall might leave his wife for her?

2. Why does Beatrice think that Marshall hasn't left his wife so far?

3. Why does Beatrice worry about what Marshall might think if he found that she'd finished the champagne by herself?

4. What would Beatrice consider hopeless?

I Love You

Althera Beryl Gray has often described the words *I love you* as the verbal equivalent of the atomic bomb. "It takes just a second to push that button," my mother says, "and then you're stuck with generations of turtles with two heads." Just so, it takes but a second to utter those words and for the next twenty-five years you're waking up next to a man who sleeps with his socks on and can only talk about basketball. In fact, says my mother, in the history of mankind, the only sentence to cause more trouble, anguish and confusion than "I love you" is "Adam, why don't you try this apple?"

The problem is that, although you know exactly what a person means when he asks you for a cup of coffee or tells you that blue isn't really your color, when that same person leans close and whispers, "I love you," nine times out of ten you have no idea what he's talking about and neither does he.

"What complete crap!" you explode. "Everyone knows what the words *I love you* mean. Even people who don't speak English know what they mean."

"Oh, yeah?" says my mother.

Example one. Martin and Molly are alone in Molly's apartment. The room is dark but for a few shreds of moonlight and the glow from the fish tank. They are more or less on the sofa, and more or less still dressed. Martin is damp with sweat and wouldn't be able to remember his phone number if it were written on his hand. Molly is having trouble regulating her breathing and has completely forgotten her mother's admonition that young ladies never raise their voices. Every hormone in the room with them is screaming, "Jump!" It is at the point where Molly's tongue starts caressing Martin that he gasps, "I love you."

Here's the question. What does Martin mean when he says, "I love you"? Does he mean that he wants to spend the rest of his life mowing Molly's lawn, or does he mean that he's enjoying her company and might like to go out for a pizza later?

Example two. Charles and Ida have been married for thirty-three years. Neither Charles nor Ida was ever very interested in sex. They did it, of course, when they were first married, because that was what you did, but eventually they tired of having to get into their pajamas and out of them and then back into them again and confined themselves to the occasional kiss on the cheek. Not that they're not close. They are close. They enjoy working in the garden together, and taking quiet walks in the countryside together, and having a cup of herbal tea in the afternoon with a cookie or two as the day draws to a gentle close.

One afternoon Charles and Ida are sipping their Red Zinger and nibbling their Lorna Doones in the living room while they watch the news. For a change, the news this afternoon is filled with doom and mayhem. Blood flows through the streets of Europe and South America and the Middle East. There are riots in the United States and bombs in Britain. Earthquakes and floods ravage the few corners of the world man hasn't managed to devastate himself. By the end of the news, there is a feeling in the room that if one were to listen closely enough one might hear the children of the planet wailing with hunger and grief. Charles reaches over and pats Ida's hand. Ida sighs. "Would you like a little more tea?" asks Ida. "I love you, old girl," says Charles. "I love you, too," says Ida. "Do you want another cookie?"

Here's the question: When Charles says, "I love you, old girl," does he mean that the last thirty-three years with Ida have given him emotional and spiritual fulfillment and that without her his life would have been devoid of meaning and passion? Or does he mean he's pretty glad he's not in Beirut? When Ida says, "I love you, too," does she mean that through her relationship with Charles she has been able to find her true self and achieve real happiness and inner peace? Or does she mean that she's also pretty glad she's not in Beirut?

Example three. While shopping in the local supermarket, Pat and Celia have a disagreement over Swiss chard. It begins when Celia says, "Ooh, we should get some Swiss chard, sweeties," and Pat says, "Not for me." Celia then says, "But you love Swiss chard, Pat. It's practically your favorite food in the world," and Pat says, "Not the way you cook it, it isn't." By the time the assistant manager comes along to tell them that if they don't stop lobbing the produce at one another the police are going to be called, the argument has left Swiss chard and is firmly lodged in Pat's childhood and selfish behavior and Celia's overbearing personality and the fact that she refuses to shave her legs. Hours later, after they get home from the station, and Celia has cried for a few hours and recalled all the other people who have criticized her overbearing personality and maltreatment of certain vegetables, and Pat has had a couple of drinks and thought a little about how lonely it must feel to live alone in a room over someone's garage with all your possessions in a couple of cardboard boxes, and they are lying on separate sides of their double bed, Pat whispers into the dark, "Celia?" "What?" Celia whispers back through her tears. "I love you, Celia," says Pat. Celia snuffles. "I love you, too," she says.

Question: Does Pat telling Celia he loves her mean that he does love her, despite the fact that she never lets him do anything he wants to do and makes him eat boiled chard when he'd rather be eating Styrofoam, or does it mean that he doesn't want to move into a room over someone's garage? Does Celia love Pat, or is she just relieved that he still wants her when she isn't quite sure that anyone else would?

It's in His Kiss

Helen and I were sitting on the patio one summer evening, talking about life and the immense complexity and excitement of the universe.

"Did I ever tell you what it was that first attracted me to Leo?" she asked me.

I tore my gaze from a distant star to look at her. "I thought it had something to do with the fact that he's thin and blond," I said. "You always go for thin, blond men. It's some sort of genetic defect."

Helen shook her head. "No, it wasn't that. I mean, I agreed to go out with him because he looked sort of human, but that's not why I decided to keep on seeing him."

"His extensive knowledge of pre-Colombian civilizations?" I ventured.

"No. The Aztecs are pretty interesting the first six or seven times you hear about them, but it wasn't that."

I sipped. If it wasn't Leo's looks or intelligence, what was the quality that had drawn the irrepressibly spirited and bohemian Helen to a man who only wore gray and considered drinking more than two glasses of wine debauched? "His prestige as a leading academic?"

"Fiddle-dee-dee," said Helen with a laugh. "You know it wasn't that."

I concentrated. I had a vague recollection that Leo once told a rather amusing joke about George Bush. "His sense of humor?"

She shook her head.

"Oh, I know," I said. "It must be his strength of character and sense of integrity."

Helen grinned. "Give up?"

I gave up.

"The first date I had with Leo was a complete disaster," Helen explained. "I mean, it wasn't that he ordered for me or used the tablecloth for a napkin or anything like that. It was just that it was boring. I can remember thinking to myself, My God, if we could bottle this guy we could make time stand still. All the way home he was yapping about some ball game the Maya used to play and I kept looking at my watch to see if it had stopped or not. I wasn't going to ask him in for coffee or anything. I was just going to thank him for a pleasant evening and say good-night and if he ever called for another date I was going to tell him I'd decided to move to Fairbanks."

"Well, I don't understand then," I said. "What happened on the drive home to change your mind?"

"Nothing," said Helen. "It happened at my door."

"At your door?"

She nodded. "He asked me if he could kiss me good-night and I was so worn down by then and eager to get inside and call my sister to tell her how the date had been that I said yes."

I nodded. "Uh huh. So then what happened?"

Helen grinned. "He kissed me."

"And that was it?"

"That was it," said Helen.

J

James Dean and Jesse James

It's no secret that obviously unsuitable men often hold a powerful allure for eminently suitable women. In fact, so unsecret is this that many experts call this the "Lady and the Outlaw Syndrome." But not my mother. My mother calls it "Settling for Frank the Accountant while Lusting after James Dean." "Or Jesse James," adds my mother. "Though, personally, I've always liked Crazy Horse."

Why are women attracted so strongly to men they know will only leave them crying in some cheap hotel room or riverbank clearing, having borrowed all their money, hocked their grandmother's earrings, and not even bothered to promise to write, assuming that they could? Is it the excitement and romance of the forbidden? The thrill of danger? The relief of knowing you'll never have to wash his socks?

"What's more interesting," says my mother, "is the fact that a woman who dreams of being carried off on the back of a sweating horse or a roaring motorcycle would be willing to drive around in Frank's BMW talking about pension schemes for the best years of her life."

I guess it's the biological female need for safety and security for reproductive purposes. No matter how blood-draining a kiss from Jesse James might be, it's not going to give you much comfort when it's snowing outside and the baby's hungry and Jesse is miles away using another name.

"It's also because no matter how good the sex, you always get something jabbed in your back when you make love on the ground," says my mother.

Jealousy

"I know Matty and I have a few problems," Ms. G told me between sobs, "but basically I'm sure he loves me."

I glanced at my notes, tapping my pen against my pad. "Matty is always criticizing you." *Tap.* "He's always complaining." *Tap.* "He's selfish and demanding." *Tap, tap.* "He has an uncontrollable temper, he hates your family and all your friends, and he never takes you out." *Tap, tap, tap.* I leaned forward on my elbows. "How can you tell that he loves you?" I asked, looking into her eyes.

She looked into mine. "Because he's insanely jealous."

I pursed my lips. "It could just be that he's insane."

For some reason, many people confuse jealousy with love, in much the way I suppose that many people confuse soap with cream cheese. Soap is white; cream cheese is white. Both soap and cream cheese are shaped like a bar. Jealousy is focused on one person; love is focused on one person. Both jealousy and love are an emotion. But soap, of course, is nothing like cream cheese, and jealousy is nothing like love.

I mentioned this to Ms. G. "Jealousy is nothing like love," I said.

"But of course it is," she protested. "It shows how much Matty needs and wants me. Like the time he followed me all the way to Minneapolis when I was going to visit my mother because he thought I wasn't really going to visit my mother but that I was going to see another man? That was because he loves me so much. He couldn't help himself."

"He followed you to Minneapolis?"

She nodded. "On the train."

"He was on the same train as you? What did you say when he showed up on the train?"

"I didn't recognize him. He was disguised as an Arab."

I tried to picture Matty Sturgeon, a tall, thin, pale, and fair-haired man of English descent, disguised as an Arab. "And what happened when you got to Minneapolis?"

Ms. G looked at me slightly blankly. "I got off the train."

"I thought you might," I said. "But then what happened?"

She made a face. "My brother-in-law was waiting to take me to my mom's."

"And did Matty go to your mom's too, or did he realize what a stupid mistake he'd made and turn around and go home?"

"I didn't actually get to my mom's," said Ms. G. And then she added by way of explanation, "Because of the accident."

"What accident?"

"The five-car pile-up."

It is physically possible to feel your heart sink. "And where was Matty the Arab during the five-car pile-up?" I inquired gently.

Ms. G gave me the tiniest and most apologetic of smiles. "He caused it."

"He caused an accident?"

"It wasn't his fault really," Ms. G protested. "He'd never met my brother-in-law, so of course he thought Ronnie was the man I'd gone to Minneapolis to see."

"Of course he did," I said. "It's a mistake anyone might make." I tapped my pencil several times. "So how did the accident happen?" I finally forced myself to ask. "Did Matty throw himself in front of the car?"

"No. He was following us in a cab."

"Well, I don't see how he could have caused an accident then. Minneapolis taxi drivers are usually pretty sensible."

"The cabbie wasn't driving," said Ms. G. "Matty was. He threw the driver out at the station."

"Back up a minute," I ordered. "Are you saying that Matty Sturgeon, doctor of medicine, doctor of psychiatry, and world-renowned creator of kinetic psychoanalysis, stole a taxi cab, chased you around Minneapolis in it, and somehow caused a five-car pile-up because he mistook your brother-in-law for your lover?"

Ms. G ignored my questions. "He started banging into the back of Ronnie's car."

I could but shake my head in wonder. "I've heard of paranoid jealous behavior before, but this really takes the prize."

"He's not usually that extreme," Ms. G defended. "I mean, he does get upset when I talk to the mailman. And once, when the guy next door helped me carry in the shopping, Matty went for him with the garden rake, but that's not that unusual, is it?"

"And you think all this proves that Matty loves you?"

"Well, what else would you call it if it isn't love?" she replied.

"Insanity?" I wondered out loud.

K

Killing Him

Very often when a relationship has ended there is still a great deal of anger and resentment left behind. Anger and resentment that can linger on for years after their object has moved to the Midwest to raise sheep. There he is, sitting in the barn, whistling a happy tune while he oversees the shearing of the sheep and thinks about whether to have pancakes or eggs for breakfast, and there you are, back in Tampa, still thinking about the time he refused to go to your family reunion and took one of his old girlfriends out dancing instead. He's shuffling back into the house, sniffing the air to see if his new wife is making pancakes or sausages this morning, the thought of you as far away as Pluto, and you're tossing and turning, sleepless with rage, muttering to yourself, "I wish I'd killed the bastard when I had the chance."

Don't wish; do it while you have the chance.

You think I'm joking, don't you?

Let's say, for example, that your longtime lover Chuck leaves you for another woman. You might have been more forgiving if the woman he left you for was a worthy competitor—Julia

Roberts, say, or Mother Teresa—but the woman he has left you for isn't. So not only are you angry, hurt, and feeling rejected, you can't believe you wasted some of the best years of your life on a man who prefers a woman who wears purple stretch pants with high heels to you. Every time you think of Chuck your stomach clenches and your body temperature rises. And you think of him all the time. Everything reminds you of him. Chocolate ice cream, Bryan Ferry songs, red hatchbacks, blue shirts, pocket-size packs of tissues, weak coffee, ginger snaps, sunshine, rain, Mondays, Tuesdays, Wednesdays, Thursdays, Fridays, Saturdays, and Sundays. . . . You stomp around talking to him under your breath. "You lentil-head," you say. "I hope your penis falls off. I hope she leaves you for someone with hair. I wouldn't give you a drink of water if I came across you in the desert dying of thirst." Passersby look at you oddly, but you don't care. You see a couple kissing at the bus stop and even though they look nothing like Chuck and his new love (he is not short and bald and she is not too skinny and revoltingly blonde) you immediately picture Chuck and her sticking their tongues into each other's mouths at another bus stop, flaunting their sex life in front of the world, and you burst into tears. At this rate, you know, you will still be crying every time you hear "These Foolish Things" ten years from now. Obviously, the only thing you can do to free yourself from Chuck is to kill him.

I call this my cathartic murder concept. What you do is, you think very carefully about killing him. You plan it in detail. Instead of wasting time and emotion picturing Chuck and Her brushing their teeth together or licking each other's legs, decide how you could kill him without bringing any suspicion on yourself, how you could make it look as though She did it. Imagine yourself telling all your friends you were going to Martha's Vineyard for the weekend. Wave them goodbye in your mind. Drive to Martha's Vineyard, listening not to Bryan Ferry singing "Smoke Gets in Your Eyes" but to Axl Rose singing "I Used to Love Her but I Had to Kill Her." Check into the hotel. Visualize yourself at the hotel desk, making a fuss about the room they gave you so they'll remember you and your alibi will be airtight. "I need to rest," you tell them. "I can't have a room right over the disco." Once in your room at the back of the hotel, you put on a girdle, a blond wig, and purple stretch pants. You don dark glasses. You sneak out of your room, down the fire escape, and out to your car, which is not your car, of course, but a rented car that is the exact model and color as Hers. You drive back to Chuck's. You know it's the night his new love has her aerobics class so he'll be alone. You still have your key. You walk in. Chuck is surprised to see you.

"What are you doing here?" he asks. He looks puzzled. He can tell something's changed in you. "Why aren't you crying?" he wants to know.

You smile. Slowly. "I've come to kill you, Chuck," you tell him. You take the gun from your pocket.

Chuck laughs. It is then that you know that he always was a fool. "Stop kidding around," he says. "Someone could get hurt with that thing."

"Someone is going to get hurt with this thing," you assure him. "For God's sake!" Chuck shrieks, suddenly aware that you're serious. "Have you lost your mind?"

"Of course not, darling," you say ever so sweetly. "I know exactly what I'm doing." You're still smiling. "First I'm going to fatally wound you," you inform him, "and then, while you're still alive and conscious, I'm going to pull off your penis with my bare hands."

"Darling," Chuck bleats. "Darling, think of what will happen to you if you do this. You'll spend the rest of your life in a lonely prison cell, playing the blues harmonica and remembering all the times we laughed together and walked in the rain. I'm begging you, not for my sake but for yours, put that gun away."

Your laughter is loud by hollow. "Not I," you say. "Your neighbors didn't see me come in here. They saw Her."

" 'Her'?" Chuck repeats, only just realizing the simple brilliance of your plan and wondering how he could ever have said he didn't think you were clever enough to mix with his architect friends. "Dana?"

"Yes," you say. "Dana. It'll be Dana who learns how to play 'Columbus Stockade' on the mouth harp, not I." You laugh again. "You'll be dead and Dana will be in solitary. Where there is no bleach."

Chuck is on his knees by now. There are tears in his eyes. He's beginning to whimper. "I'll come back," he says. "You were right. This thing with Dana was just a midlife crisis. I know that now. You're the only woman I've ever really loved. I'll come back and we'll get married and we'll honeymoon in Atlantic City, just like you always wanted."

And that's when you let him have it. "Bye, bye, Chuck," you say. "I'm never going to think of you again."

"Just a minute, Serena," says my mother. "There's one little flaw in this cathartic murder concept of yours."

I'd been hoping she wouldn't notice, but, of course, she's right. At the point in the fantasy where Chuck starts whimpering and tells you you're the only woman he ever loved and that he wants to marry you and take you to watch low tide in Atlantic City for a week, you're liable to weaken, put the gun down, and hurl yourself into his arms.

"Women!" says my mother. "It's always so difficult to know what they really want."

116

L

Leave Him, Don't Love Him

How You Can Tell When You've Had Enough

One of the most-used tools of the professional relationship crisis counselor is something we call the Big Why? No matter what the tale—whether he loved you too much or not enough, whether he liked to have sex while wearing a wet suit and singing "A Whiter Shade of Pale" or didn't like to have sex more than once a year—at the end of every tear-streaked story there is really only one question to ask: Why? Why did you move in with him if you knew what he was like? Why do you stay with him? Why can't you leave?

And it isn't long before the professional relationship crisis counselor realizes that though every now and then the answer to the Big Why? is "Because he's richer than the Queen of England" or "Because he's blackmailing me" or "Because he'll shoot my dog if I go," nine times out of ten the answer is "Because I love him."

It is well nigh impossible to reason with someone who's convinced she's in love. "I know he's a bum," says Suzanne. "He cheats on me, he disappears for weeks, he sold my car, he broke my bust of Jim Morrison, and he didn't even send me a get-well card when I got hit by that bicycle, but what can I do?" She shrugs. She sighs. She looks at you with helpless eyes. "I love him," says Suzanne. "So what can I do?"

"Dump the dork," says my mother. She snorts, contemptuously. "Love and insanity are the two things that allow a person to get away with murder," says my mother. She snorts again. "Staying with someone who makes you unhappy is not love," says my mother. "It's like only eating food that makes you sick."

But how do we convince ourselves of that? How can you tell when what you're feeling isn't love but nausea?

To help you decide when it's time to stop loving him and start leaving him, my mother and I have come up with a list of telltale signs. Any one of these signs should alert you to the fact that the gas has run out of the car of your relationship and you're the one who's pushing it uphill. More than one sign? You're not pushing, the car's rolling back down the hill and dragging you with it.

1. *You talk about X all the time, even to people you don't know.*

For instance: You and a work mate are traveling to Atlanta on the train together. You and this work mate know each other to exchange superficial pleasantries but you are not what one would call intimate. On the train ride to Atlanta, this person, searching around for something to follow your conversation on Vatican reform, says, "So, how are things?" To which you instantly reply, "Well, not so good if you want to know the truth. I haven't been the same since X had that scene with the hula dancer."

"X?" says your companion? "Who's X?"

You spend the next four hours telling her who X is. By the end of the trip, she knows more about X than X does.

Even a girl who loves someone usually spares strangers the gorier details of her lover's problems with his mother.

2. You talk about X all the time, no matter what everyone else is talking about.

For instance . . . you and your friends go to the new Harrison Ford movie. Afterwards you stop for a drink. "Wasn't that a great movie?" asks one of your friends.

"Isn't Harrison Ford absolutely gorgeous?" asks another.

"Did I tell you what X said last night?" ask you.

A person who loves another person can still appreciate cultural experiences such as a good movie. And only a person who is nauseated all the time could fail to appreciate Harrison Ford.

3. You never shut up about X.

For instance, your best friend, an actress, comes to tell you that she has just had the career break she's been working toward for nearly two decades. After all the years of repertory, all the years of provincial theater, all the years of voice-overs, walk-ons, and waiting on tables, she's landed a major part in a big series. Your best friend is the happiest you've seen her in a long time. Her cheeks are flushed, her eyes are bright, she can't stop grinning. You listen to her burble on, nodding and smiling and sipping your wine, and when she finally stops talking you burst into tears and say, "I really think X is having an affair, Chris. I really do."

An inability to relate to anyone else is not an indication of great passion but of emotional influenza.

4. Whenever something goes wrong between you and X, you take the blame.

For instance, X forgets to pick you up after work, as arranged. When you finally make your way through the blizzard, carrying the twenty-five pound weights that you bought for X on the bus, X is sitting at home, impersonating something that grows from the couch. You say a few sharpish words to him and he storms off into the storm. He doesn't come home that night. He doesn't come home the next.

119

When he does come home, he tells you that he's moving in with another woman.

Your first reaction is not to try to remove his penis. Your first reaction is to say to yourself, "If only I'd called him to remind him to pick me up at the office, none of this would ever have happened."

People in love do not say "Maybe if," "If only," or "I should've" more than once a year, and then it's usually in relation to where they parked the car.

5. Your friends start suggesting that you listen to yourself.

"Listen to yourself," they said. "We asked you if you wanted to come to Trinidad with us for the weekend and you said you have to wait and see if X is going to be around. Last week we invited you out for black bean salsa and you wouldn't come because you thought X might call."

But you don't listen to yourself. You say, "I don't know what you're talking about. He might be around this weekend. He might have called the other night."

A refusal to let even the smallest glimmer of reality seep through the blinds of your mind has as much to do with love as trees have to do with air pollution.

6. You are terrified of going anywhere, no matter how briefly, in case you miss X.

For instance, you buy a cellular phone to avoid any possibility of missing his call. Just in case he should call. The time you used to spend worrying that he was calling you while you were stuck in traffic you now spend worrying that the batteries are dead.

Being afraid to go down the road for a container of milk because you might miss his call is not as bad as buying three extension cords so you can bring the phone from downstairs upstairs into the bathroom with you in case he calls while you're in the shower, or refusing free tickets to a Springsteen concert because you can't be away from a phone for three hours, but it's close.

7. *You lie to yourself shamelessly.*

"I was right!" you tell your best friend. "He was having an affair. With my cousin Linda."

Your best friend nods, not so much understandingly as knowingly. "So I guess this means the wedding's off," she says.

You shake your head. "Oh no," you say. "No, the wedding's not off. We talked it over and we're closer now than we were before. You know, I think he really needed that last fling."

Your best friend stares at you over her teacup. "Listen to yourself," says your best friend.

"What?" say you.

A steadfast refusal to listen to yourself could mean that the disease is actually eroding your brain.

8. *Your friends start telling you to leave him.*

Every time you recount another X story your friends say, "Leave him."

"You're right," you say. "I know you're right. He's not worth it."

"He isn't worth it," say your friends. "The man's a bigger waste of time than reading the *Enquirer.* Jack the jerk."

"I'm going to," you say. "I am. Did I tell you that he threw the kettle through the kitchen window?"

"Drop the dope," say your friends. "Don't put up with him for one more minute."

You glance at your watch. "Gee," you say, "I'd better go. X really hates it when I'm late getting home."

"Geez," say your friends. "Will you listen to yourself?"

A continuing steadfast refusal to listen to yourself is the equivalent of a self-lobotomization.

9. *Strangers start asking you what you see in him.*

"That's him?" they say. "What on earth do you see in him?"

Your friends understand that you don't see anything in X— after all, he has the sense of fun of Stalin and less personality than a piece of quartz, what's to see?—you just think that you're just in love with him. But you're not sure how to explain this to a stranger.

If you can't explain to someone who doesn't actually know what a complete turkey X is what it is you see in him—that is if you can't even make something up, like he's a great lover or his toes are webbed—then you're not in love, you're dicing with death.

10. *You forgive him anything.*

As an example: You and X go to the Bahamas for two weeks. You have a wonderful time. The fire is rekindled, the furnace of love restored. When you arrive at the airport back home, still warm and glowing and smelling faintly of coconut and rum, X says, "Wait here, love, I'll get a cart." That's the last you see of X for five weeks.

Five weeks later, when you're telling your best friend that X has phoned wanting to know if his plaid boxers are at your house, your best friend says, "I hope you told him what he could do with his lousy shorts," says your friend.

You don't say anything.

"Oh, don't tell me!" screams your best friend. "You washed them, ironed them, and took them over to him, didn't you?"

You don't say anything.

"Listen to yourself!" roars your best friend.

"But I wasn't saying anything," you say.

A growing lack of any sense of pride or dignity indicates that you would have been better off checking yourself into the hospital than going to the Bahamas.

11. *You start alienating your friends.*

One night, your best friend takes you out for a drink. Over your second white wine, your best friend says, "There's something I have to tell you. This is very difficult for me, and I know it's going to hurt you, but I can't see you going on, deluding yourself about X anymore."

You say, "Nothing you can say will surprise me, Chris. Not

122

after the way he behaved in Mystic. Did I tell you what he did in Mystic?"

Chris says, "Please, just listen to me. Just this once. I'm begging you."

"I can't believe I didn't tell you about Mystic," you say. "I haven't cried so much since the Christmas he went away without me."

Your best friend leans forward so your faces almost touch. "Last Saturday at your birthday party, X made a pass at me!" she screams. She sits back. "There," she says. "I said it."

It takes a few second for this to sink in.

"What?" you say.

She repeats her announcement that your boyfriend made a pass at her, this time a trifle more calmly. She tells you what she said and what X said and how he tried to get his hand down her blouse.

"Now will you dump this dweeb?" she asks when she's through.

You respond to this question by throwing your wine at your best friend, and inform the rest of the bar that she is a slut and a whore and a woman who makes Judas Iscariot look reliable. You keep seeing X, but you never speak to Chris again.

A person willing to sacrifice her friends for her boyfriend had better pray that the illness isn't a fatal one or there'll be no one to attend the funeral—because you can bet your last tissue that he'll have a date.

12. *You begin to fantasize revenge on him.*

For instance, you fantasize that you and X have finally gone your separate ways even though, at the end, he begged you to give him just one more chance (his 978th). Years later, you and X meet at a party. You look better than you have ever looked in your life, you're wealthy, you're famous, and you're with one of the most handsome, richest, and most charismatic men who ever set foot on the planet. You smile at X as you

123

sail past him, but it is not a smile without malice. You can hear his heart breaking as you lean against your new lover and laugh warmly.

Anyone not in a state of delirium (anyone but you, that is) could see that love has been replaced with a potent virus. You don't see this, though. You're still trying to convince yourself that the heat you feel is from his embrace and not the fever.

13. *You become violent.*

During your last argument with X, you found yourself standing in the doorway, screaming at the top of your lungs, "I hope your car crashes. I hope the ambulance is too late to save you!" What is most disturbing about this is not the fact that the entire block heard you, but that you really meant it.

People who love other people do not want them to die, no matter how angry they are with them.

14. *Your friends start exhibiting signs of compassion fatigue.*

Instead of nodding sympathetically and reaching for the salsa and tortilla chips every time you start complaining about how badly X treats you, they change the subject to endangered species or people they know with a chronic illness.

Loving someone and being a bore about them are not even remotely similar.

15. *More serious indications of compassion fatigue begin to surface.*

People—people like your new best friend and your mother—stop inviting you over for deluxe pizza and beer. In fact, they stop inviting you over for anything. When you do manage to surprise one of them into answering the phone and invite yourself to visit, the first thing she says is, "But not if you're going to talk about X."

If even your mother, the woman who lied to you about your hips and your chin and Santa Claus for all those years, won't lie to you about X, you're not just nauseated, you're close to dead.

Leaving Him Alone

Many women who have a man are reluctant to leave him alone for any length of time. There are several reasons for this lack of confidence in the male of the species to survive for an indefinite period.

The first, of course, is that they can never find anything once you've left. Your car is just pulling away from your curb and your mind is on the gray skies of New York, where you'll be spending a few days visiting friends, when you hear the heavens shouting your name. "Baby!" the heavens are crying. "Baby! Stop!" You stop at the corner and look back. There's your cohabitor racing down the street after you, shouting, "Baby! Baby! Where are my keys? Where's the corkscrew? Where's the coffee? Have you left me anything to eat?"

The second, of course, is that they can never do anything once you've left. You've just arrived in Cambodia on a fact-finding mission for the U.N., and the first thing that greets you is a slightly hysterical fax from your cohabitor asking where the instructions for the washing machine are. I have to wash my tennis shoes for the match on Saturday, it says. How in hell do I turn the damn thing on? It's got more knobs and buttons than a space shuttle. Answer by return fax. Situation desperate.

The third reason, of course, is that when you return home, you won't be able to find anything either. No corkscrew, no large spoons, no oven mitts. The jars and plastic containers you have been saving for years will all have been thrown out. The pantry and the refrigerator will be empty. There'll be one sheet of toilet paper left in the house. The cat will be using shredded newspaper. The shriveled brown thing stuck to the bottom of the iron will later be identified as a sock he tried to iron. The sheets will all be blue.

And the fourth reason . . . ?

Leaving Him Alone, the Fourth Reason Not to—A Case Study

When Miriam came to see me she was extremely distraught. Her life was collapsing around her. The past gave her nightmares. The future made her break out in a cold sweat. Miriam's story was not unusual. She and Ben had been living together for several years in relative companionship and contentment. They'd decorated the living room, bought carpeting for the hall, and were talking about either having a child or getting a dog in the not-too-distant future. All was well. And then Miriam went away for a week.

MIRIAM: Ever since that week in Cambodia, my whole world has been turned upside down. I can't eat, I can't sleep, I can't stop weeping. . . .

S.G.: I take it something on the catastrophic side happened in your absence.

MIRIAM: [sobbing uncontrollably] Umph.

S.G.: What did he do? Kill your dog? Sell your jewelry? Burn down the house? Move to Ontario? Buy a motorcycle? [Ed. note: These are all well-documented possibilities.]

MIRIAM: No. He couldn't find the bread knife.

S.G.: Excuse me?

MIRIAM: He couldn't find the bread knife. He didn't have time to shop because he works all day, and he has his softball on Monday nights, and his favorite TV show is on Tuesday, and Wednesday's squash, and Thursday he likes to relax. . . . Well, anyway, he had to use the bread that was already in the freezer. You know, the bread that I'd bought.

S.G.: And?

MIRIAM: And it wasn't sliced. You see, Ben likes his toast thick, and he loves grilled sandwiches, so I always buy unsliced bread.

126

S.G.: And that was why he needed the knife?

MIRIAM: That's right. Only he couldn't find it. He thought that he was going to starve to death.

S.G.: Why couldn't Ben find the knife? Where was it?

MIRIAM: In the drawer.

S.G.: Um, when you say in the drawer, Miriam, which drawer do you mean? The drawer in the bathroom? In the garage? In the study?

MIRIAM: No, of course not. Why would I keep the bread knife in the bathroom? I mean the drawer in the kitchen.

S.G.: It was in the drawer in the kitchen and Ben couldn't find it?

MIRIAM: That's right. Actually, I'm not really sure that he knew what it looked like. I mean, he hadn't seen it much, since he never sliced the bread. Anyway, there he was with nothing to eat and all this bread, and he couldn't find the bread knife. So he called my sister.

S.G.: Um, Miriam, excuse me, but could we just backtrack here for a minute? When you say there was nothing to eat, do you mean that the only thing in the house was unsliced, frozen bread?

MIRIAM: Oh, no. There were a lot of things in the fridge and the pantry. The problem was that Ben had used the last frozen dinner for a midnight snack the day before I left. Because we didn't know I was going. Originally I was supposed to leave the following week, but there was an emergency, and anyway I didn't have time to do the shopping as I would have normally and that's why there was nothing in the freezer but bread.

S.G.: What are you saying, Miriam? Are you saying that Ben, a thirty-five-year-old professor of physics, can't cook himself a meal?

127

MIRIAM: You know, it's funny, but that's just what my sister said, and in that exact same tone. But you're both wrong. Ben can cook. Just nothing hot.

S.G.: Nothing hot.

MIRIAM: Right. So anyway, Ben called my sister and asked her if she knew where I keep the bread knife. My sister knew where I keep the bread knife, of course, because she comes over all the time and has lunch and supper, and she always gives me a hand, so of course she knew. But she wouldn't tell Ben.

S.G.: She wouldn't?

MIRIAM: [shaking her head] No. She gets like that sometimes. It's because she's a Scorpio. So then Ben called my mother.

S.G.: And does your mother know where you keep the bread knife?

MIRIAM: Oh, absolutely. She visits a lot, too. But she wouldn't tell him either.

S.G.: Why not? Is she also a Scorpio?

MIRIAM: No, she's a Libra. But she said Ben reminded her too much of my father. My father's been driving my mother crazy for thirty-nine years.

S.G.: I see. What happened then?

MIRIAM: He called my boss.

S.G.: Ben called your boss? I'm surprised he didn't call his mother. She might have been able to make a good guess.

MIRIAM: Oh, he couldn't call his mother. She's always nagging him because he's just like his father. Ben's father ate out every night for a week when Ben's mother went to Dallas with her bridge club because he couldn't find the can opener. She'd have had a cow if she found out Ben didn't know where the bread knife was.

S.G.: So he called your boss. And would your boss tell him where the bread knife was?

128

MIRIAM: She only eats take-out, so she didn't have a clue. By then poor Ben was practically fainting from hunger, of course.

S.G.: He might as well have been in Cambodia. What did he do then?

MIRIAM: He went next door, to Ava's.

S.G.: And did Ava know where the bread knife was?

MIRIAM: [bursting into renewed tears] She made him lasagne.

S.G.: Lasagne?

MIRIAM: [through her sobs] With meat sauce. And then she told him she thought it was really petty of me not to slice the bread for him before I left. She said she couldn't believe I would neglect a great guy like Ben in that way. And then she went to bed with him.

S.G.: No wonder you're so upset. Your anger and hurt and sense of betrayal by Ben are completely understandable.

MIRIAM: [gulping and snuffling] Oh, it's not Ben I'm angry and upset with. It's Ava.

S.G.: Ava?

MIRIAM: Uh huh. She was one of my very best friends. We were going to go to Africa together. I can't believe she'd do a thing like that to me.

Letter Bombs

It was Ellie Mortimer who first postulated the Letter Bomb Theory. "Every time I think of Artie I think of letter bombs," she said.

"You mean you want to send him one?" I asked.

"After the way he carried on at that disco in D.C. I wouldn't mind sending him a package bomb," said Ellie. "Or a MIRV. But no, that's not what I meant."

Picture yourself sitting at home. You have a pleasant life—nice friends, agreeable companionship with your cats—but you can't help feeling that something's missing. And then one day, as you are sitting there, the mail arrives. You hurry out to collect it. There are a few threatening brown envelopes, there's a letter from your mother on which she's scrawled OPEN ME FIRST, there are three requests for money for irrigation projects, a rose catalogue, and the news that you've won either a million dollars or a port decanter. And one expensive pearl-gray envelope with your name and address impeccably, not to say elegantly, written in purple ink. What could it be? You've never had a letter quite like this before. It has class. It has mystery. It has a certain allure. You begin to imagine all kinds of mind-boggling, life-changing possibilities. Romantic adventures . . . fantastic opportunities . . . spiritual fulfillment . . . poetry and love . . . "Wow!" you exclaim. "This is something really special. This could be the thing that's missing in my life!"

You hurry back inside, you throw the bills and the junk mail on the table, you sit down, trying to control your breathing. Normally you rip apart your mail like a hound ripping apart a rabbit, but not this time. Slowly, deliciously, tenderly savoring each second of anticipation, you carefully open the exquisite envelope. Your heart pounds, your blood races. As your fingers give the final pull you think to yourself This is it. . . . This is the thing I've been waiting for. . . . And then the damn thing explodes in your face and twenty minutes later the riot squad are scraping you off the floor.

"Do you see what I'm getting at?" asked Ellie.

"I think so," I said.

You go along for months, even years, meeting men who are about as interesting as a a letter from your accountant or a seed catalogue, and then one day you come across this pearl-gray envelope of a man. He's attractive, he's intriguing, he has a sense of humor and a flat stomach. You think, Hey, this one's really nice. You ask him a few telling questions. You discover that you both like the blues, Kurt Vonnegut novels, Mexican food, and thirties comedies. You can't see anything really wrong with him.

He's not patronizing, he's not overly fussy, he's not fatiguingly aggressive or demanding, he doesn't live with his mother, talk about his ex-wife all the time, or obsess about his hairline, he seems to be capable of speech and self-expression. You think, Hey, this one is all right. At last I've found a man I can have an equal and working relationship with. At last I've found a man who isn't full of secret phobias. A man who speaks. Your imagination starts to play havoc with your hormones—and vice versa. You picture the two of you strolling through the Grand Canyon together. You picture popcorn fights while you watch videos till dawn. When he asks you to move in with him you don't even hesitate. And then you wake up a few months later in the middle of the night and he's standing on the foot of the bed, just staring at you in the dark, and when you ask him what's wrong he accuses you of being like his mother.

"Exactly," said Ellie. "He goes off in your face just like a letter bomb, and the next thing you know your friends are scraping you off the floor again."

Letting Go

Jane and I were sitting in the kitchen one afternoon, drinking tea and talking about life. I finished explaining my theory about Hamlet to her, and looked over at her for comment. People find my theory about Hamlet very stimulating.

Jane was breaking off a piece of cookie. "Seen Drew lately?" she asked, her eyes on the scattering crumbs.

For some reason, I'd assumed the first name out of her mouth might be Polonius or Gertrude.

"Drew?"

She popped the piece of cookie into her mouth. "Um," said Janet.

"You don't mean Drew Highwayman, do you?" I sighed, tetchily. Like the rest of Jane's friends, I was suffering from an extreme case of Drew Highwayman overload. Two years of discussing where he might be, what he might be thinking, what he might be dreaming, what he might be saying, what he might be doing, and whom he might be doing it with had taken their toll. "I thought you said last week that you were finally ready to let go of Drew."

Jane reached for another cookie. "I am," she said. "I don't sit outside his house anymore, do I? I don't phone him all the time. I don't follow him after work. It's been months since the last time I tried to run him off the road."

"Then why are you asking if I've seen him?"

"No special reason. I was just thinking that he lives in your neighborhood and you do have a lot of mutual friends . . . so I thought that maybe you had seen him, that's all."

"But you don't care anymore, Jane," I reminded her. "You've let go. You live in a Drew Highwaymanless world."

"Of course I do, Serena." She shrugged. She smiled. "You don't have to worry about me. I'm over him completely now, I really am. Totally and completely. Everything you said was true. I've thrown out all the things that might remind me of him—the sheets, the bug light in the yard, the electric can opener, the old phone books, even that pack of dried seaweed we bought together in Chinatown. I'm free, Serena, free as a bird."

"You're sure you don't mean as free as a chicken?"

Jane's laughter ricocheted through the kitchen. She shook her head. "Over him," she said. "Totally and completely cured." She dunked half a cookie into her tea. "I'm amazed I even remember his name."

"What's his hat size? Which part of the paper does he always read first?"

"I don't remember, Serena. I'm pretending he's dead, just like your mom suggested."

"I haven't seen him."

She eyed me shrewdly over her soggy cookie. "Really? I would have thought you would have bumped into each other at the Flowers' barbecue."

132

I put my cup down. "How did you know about the Flowers'
barbecue? It was a last-minute thing."

"And did you see him there?"

"No one knew about the Flowers' barbecue, Jane. They didn't
know themselves until a few hours before."

"So you did see him there."

"Not to speak to."

"Was he with anyone?"

"Jane, I didn't speak to him."

"You can tell me, Serena. I won't be upset. Was he with the
short blonde or the skinny brunette?"

"Jane, I just caught the quickest glimpse of him down at the
bottom of the lawn."

She helped herself to more tea. "What did he say?"

"Jane, he didn't say anything. He was miles away. We didn't
even nod to each other."

She stirred slowly. "He didn't ask about me?"

"Jane, I told you, I didn't speak to him."

"He didn't say anything about me? Was it because he was
with the blonde? She looks like the bossy type. I bet he would
have asked about me if she hadn't been with him."

"Jane!" I slammed my cup down. "Drew Highwayman is dead,
remember? D-e-a-d. I don't want to hear one more word about
him, do you understand? Not one more word."

Jane stared silently across the table at me, thinking, letting
go. At last she spoke. "If he were dead, do you think he'd want
me at the funeral?" she asked.

Lies Men Tell Women

The Three Best

I'll call you tomorrow.

I hardly know her.

I won't come in your mouth.

133

The Next Three

I didn't mean for it to happen like this.
Size isn't important.
Of course I know what I'm doing.

Lies Women Tell Men

The First Four

It was wonderful.
I've never experienced anything like that before.
I never want to see you again.
Of course I'm not going to tell anyone.

The Second

I was in the shower.
It was on sale.
My mother knows nothing about it.
I thought you knew.

Listen to Yourself

To paraphrase Robert Burns, if we could see ourselves as others
see us we wouldn't have half the problems that we do have. Or,
to go him one better, if you could hear yourself as you hear others you would never have wasted two years of our life on the
accordion player who talked to Elvis or on the defrocked priest.

A Conversation With Yourself

YOURSELF: He didn't call.

YOU: Who didn't call?

YOURSELF: Bill. He said he'd give me a call, so I waited in all weekend and he never called.

YOU: You're kidding, right? You stayed in all weekend, waiting for Bill to call? Again?

YOURSELF: At least sitting around the house for two days gave me plenty of time to think.

YOU: If you had any more time to think you'd be able to solve the world's problems.

YOURSELF: I can see now that it's all my fault.

YOU: Global warming?

YOURSELF: Bill. I can see now that I was too demanding. I wasn't understanding enough of his needs and feelings.

YOU: Have you been straying too close to the petro-chemical plant again? You bent over backward considering Bill's needs and feelings. You gave up a chance to go to Hawaii so you could spend time with Bill. You got rid of the cat because he was allergic. You let him drop by with his buddies at three in the morning. You loaned him your car. You didn't complain when he went to Tidewater, Maine, for three weeks and never sent you a postcard. You even learned to prepared sushi because it's his favorite food, and you can't stand fish. How much more understanding do you think you could have been?

YOURSELF: You're right. It wasn't that I was too demanding. It was that I wasn't demanding enough. Bill's one of those men who needs to be dominated.

YOU: What, with a whip and a chair?

135

YOURSELF: You can joke all you want, but I can see now exactly where I went wrong. He expects women to tell him what to do. I should have bossed him around more. I should have kept him guessing.

YOU: Guessing about what?

YOURSELF: Guessing about whether I liked him or not. You know what men are like, if you're too eager they lose interest. They like to be strung along. The worse you treat them, the better they act. Maybe I should have gone to that awards ceremony on Saturday night after all. Then Bill would have been sure to call and he would have been jealous because I wasn't there and I might be out with another man.

YOU: Wait a minute, I thought you said you wanted a mature, adult relationship, not one built on games and subterfuge.

YOURSELF: Do you think he might have called while I was in the shower?

M

Male Behavior

Lilah and I were sitting in her kitchen, playing five-hundred rummy and talking about life.

"Have you ever noticed how men say one thing and mean another?" she asked me.

"You mean how they're always carrying on about peace but they never stop making war?"

She picked up six cards. "Not exactly."

"You mean like Jimmy Swaggart, preaching against sin and then visiting prostitutes?"

She threw down a seven. "You're getting closer."

"Oh, I know what you're getting at. You mean how they tell you they love you and then they make a pass at your best friend."

Lilah shook her head. "Kind of."

"You mean how they tell you they can't live without you and then they take a job in Ohio?"

She laid out the aces. "Not just that. I meant more like they tell you that they'd rather die than end up with a woman like their mother, and then you marry them and right away they want to know why your pot roast doesn't taste like their mom's and they can't remember how to wash their own socks."

"We're not talking about Alan again, are we?" I asked. At last count, Lilah and I had been talking about Alan for twelve years.

"I can see now that I never really understood Alan," said Lilah, who had said this before. "I thought we were two sides of the same coin. Two peas in the same pod. Two leaves from the same tree."

Two heads of the same monster, I almost said, but thought better of it. "So alike it was a crime to waste two houses on you," I said instead, quoting my mother.

"Exactly," said Lilah. "But I was wrong."

So was my mother. Instead of being so alike it was a crime to waste two houses on them, Lilah and Alan were so unalike that it was a minor miracle that they'd landed on the same planet, and mind-boggling that they'd ever gotten any further than "Where would you like to go to eat?"

"Not only weren't we in the same pod, we weren't even on the same plant."

When Lilah met Alan they were both struggling young artists living in squalor on canned beans and toast. Alan made it clear right from the start that he didn't want to be part of a mortgage-oriented, two-point-five-children-and-a-small-dog couple. He wanted to experience Life, not hang around in the foyer waiting for it to begin. He wanted to soar. Lilah couldn't have agreed more. "I'm a free spirit, too," she told him. "The last thing I want is to be tied down."

Alan proposed at the end of three months. Lilah said, "We're free spirits, Alan, we don't need a marriage certificate."

But as soon as they were married, Alan began to change. He wanted real dinners. He left his socks on the floor. He could never find his keys. He didn't like the way Lilah dressed. He started sentences with the phrase "My mother never . . ." He got a job. He took out a mortgage. When Lilah asked him why they couldn't go on living in squalor and being free spirits, he accused her of having an affair with the sculptor downstairs.

"You did turn out to have different goals," I said cautiously.

"Like Einstein and Hitler." She rolled her eyes. "I should never have married him," said Lilah. "But what could I do? Remember when he came back from California because I was going to go to Montreal for a few months? Remember when he begged me to marry him?"

"I remember," I said. "He threatened to pin a note to his chest that said Lilah Berkhop drove me to this and throw himself off an overpass."

"I should have let him," said Lilah. "The blood would probably have blotted out my name."

"He wouldn't have done it," I pointed out.

"You're right," she said. "He never did anything else he said he'd do. Why should he have done that?"

Male Ego

Sally and Shane have been seeing each other for a few weeks, in a casual though not totally unamorous way. Tonight they are sitting in the kitchen, talking about life.

"So then, in 1988, I decided to completely change my life and I quit my job and retrained as a CPA," Shane is saying. "Although I have a very logical, orderly mind and have always been especially gifted at math, I'm also a very people-oriented kind of person and I thought this would give me the greatest opportunity to use all my talents." He glances at his cup. "You wouldn't have a little more coffee in that pot, would you, Sally?" he asks.

Sally, who started to doze during 1982, when Shane went to Massachusetts, fell in love with a bisexual ice skater, broke his ankle, and read Hemingway for the first time, jumps to her feet. "I'll make some fresh," she says.

"Oh, I didn't mean for you to go to any trouble," says Shane, "but as you're up you wouldn't have a few more cookies, too, would you?"

139

"I think I've still got some peanut butter cookies," says Sally as she puts the water into the coffee maker.

"Peanut butter?"

Sally notices the unhappy expression that settles on Shane's lips. Quelling the unkind thought that this is the first time anything has had a chance to settle on Shane's lips in the past four hours since he's been talking so much, Sally says, " 'Fraid so."

"Aren't there any sandwich cookies left?" asks Shane.

Sally shakes her head. Shane's expression changes from merely unhappy to that of a man whose finest dreams have turned to dust.

"If you're hungry I guess I could fix you a sandwich or something," says Sally.

"I don't like cold food late at night," says Shane. "It gives me indigestion."

"Scrambled eggs?" suggests Sally. "Grilled cheese? Soup?"

"You wouldn't have a little pasta in the cupboard, would you?"

"Pasta?" asks Sally.

"Not that brown stuff, though," says Shane. "It sticks to my teeth."

"Pasta?" Sally repeats. "Now?"

"With tomato sauce if you've got any," says Shane. "But plain tomato sauce. Nothing too spicy."

Sally begins her search for pasta and plain, unspicy tomato sauce.

"So where was I?" asks Shane.

Sally gets down on the floor, peering into the dark recesses of the cupboard under the counter. "Around 1988," Sally doesn't say as much as grunt.

Shane nods. "Right—1988. Well, while I was doing my accountancy course, I met Carmella. She was Italian. Very beautiful and sensuous . . . you know what Italian women are like . . . , but very temperamental, too. Carmella broke my heart. . . ."

While Shane describes, in detail, how Carmella Armatutti broke his heart in 1988, Sally climbs up on the sink so she can reach the top shelf of the cupboard.

"And then you know what she said?" Shane is saying as Sally falls off the sink. "She said I was a lousy kisser. She said my tongue was short and soulless."

"How's this?" asks Sally, staggering back to her feet with a can of tomato sauce in one hand and a box of spaghetti in the other.

"It's green," says Shane.

"It's all I have," says Sally.

"I never told her what I thought of the racket she made every time she had an orgasm, did I? I didn't tell her she sounded like someone was slaughtering a pig."

"So the green spaghetti's all right?" asks Sally, checking her knee to see if it's bleeding.

"It'll have to do," says Shane. "The worst thing was that we'd have these violent fights and we'd break up and then she'd suddenly turn up on my doorstep in tears." He sighs. "You know what she did one time?"

While Sally fixes the pasta, Shane tells her what Carmella did one time.

"So in 1989 I threw myself into my work to get over her," Shane is saying as Sally sets his meal in front of him. "It wasn't easy— accountancy is a lot trickier than most people imagine, it isn't just adding up a few figures on a calculator, but after Carmella went back to Rochester the minutes seemed like hours and the days seemed like years. You know how time can just seem to stand still?"

"Oh, I know," says Sally. She pours them both more coffee.

Caught, perhaps, by the heartfelt sincerity in her voice, Shane looks over at her. "Aren't you having any spaghetti?" he asks.

Sally starts to say that she doesn't usually eat spaghetti after midnight, but Shane cuts her off. "Don't tell me," he tells her. "You're on a diet." He smiles. "That was another thing about Carmella, she had the most incredible figure, but she never had to diet."

"How nice for her," says Sally.

"I guess that's why I've always liked Julia Roberts," says Shane. "She has a body very similar to Carmella's."

"I've always liked Nicolas Cage," says Sally.

141

Caught, perhaps, by the sharp emotion in her voice, Shane looks over at her. "Nicolas Cage? What are you talking about you've 'always liked Nicolas Cage'?"

Suffering slightly from sleep deprivation and some explicit descriptions of Carmella Armatutti's love-making, Sally says, "You know, I've always liked him. He's cute. I think he's probably an incredibly tender and sensitive lover. I imagine his kisses must feel like the breath of butterflies as they run down your body."

"Nicolas Cage?" Shane repeats. "Are you saying that the reason I don't get more than a kiss at the door is because of that funny-looking pseudoactor? Are you saying you're more attracted to Nicolas Cage than you are to me?"

"Uffg," says Sally, her mouth filled with coffee.

Shane scrapes back his chair. "Well that's that then, isn't it?" he asks. "Why don't you make me feel like a cow pie, Sally? Why don't you stomp on my feelings and trample them into the ground?"

"For heaven's sake, Shane," says Sally, "sit down and finish your spaghetti."

Shane's voice is thick with emotion. "I will not sit down and finish my spaghetti, Sally. You've gone too far this time."

Sally runs down the hallway after him. "Shane, come back. Please. I'm sorry, I really am."

"Well . . ." says Shane. He follows her back to the kitchen. He sits down. "Don't you have any cheese?" he asks.

Maturity

There is an old saying, passed down from mother to daughter, generation after generation, that tells you all you need to know about the male maturation process.

And this is it: Men don't grow up, they grow bald.

Maybe-If—The Game

Whatever you do when a relationship is over, don't start playing the Maybe-If Game. Maybe if I hadn't refused to go brass rubbing with him . . . Maybe if I'd shown him how to use the washer . . . Maybe if I hadn't been so angry the time he was six hours late for a dinner party he'd arranged . . . Maybe if I hadn't been ill for that month . . . The Maybe-If Game, like the Should've Game (I should've been more understanding . . . I should've let him keep his motorcycle in my kitchen . . . I should've given him a three-hundredth chance . . .), is no more than an exercise in futility. You didn't and you can't. Or, as my mother likes to say, "Maybe if you'd had the brains you were born with you wouldn't have gone out with him in the first place."

Meeting Bob Dylan

A Cautionary Tale of Obsessive Love

It was on a stormy Thursday night that Samantha Greenwall first came to a meeting of the group. At last—after years of rationalization and denial, after months of tears and excuses—she was finally ready and able to admit the truth about herself and ask for help, understanding, and support.

When it was Samantha's turn to introduce herself, she got shakily to her feet and looked around the crowded room, pulling nervously on the sleeve of her shirt. She cleared her throat. "My name is Samantha Greenwall," she said quietly. She looked at me and I smiled my encouragement. Again, she cleared her throat. She raised her chin. Her voice became stronger. "My name is Samantha Greenwall," she repeated. "And I'm a Sucker for Love."

As Samantha began to haltingly tell her story, my mind went back six months to the first time she visited my office. . . .

"Good afternoon, Ms. Greenwall," I'd said as she entered the room. "Won't you sit down?"

Samantha Greenwall, a tall, statuesque redhead in her midthirties, had smiled shyly and sat in the chair in front of my desk. "Thank you," she'd said.

"Now, let me see . . ." I'd begun, glancing at the letter she'd written asking for an emergency session. "It says here that your boyfriend's left you and none of your family or friends will speak to you anymore."

She'd snuffed back a tar. "That's right," she'd whispered. "I . . . I have no one left."

I'd hazarded a guess based not on what she'd told me—which was nothing—but on my years of professional experience. "This wouldn't be because of an addiction to romance, would it? This wouldn't be because you're so emotionally needy that all you have to hear is one chorus of 'Stand by Your Man' and you turn into yogurt?"

Samantha had snuffed. "Oh, no," she'd answered quickly. "It's nothing like that. It's because of Bob Dylan."

Bob Dylan? My eyes had gone back to the letter. She mentioned losing her boyfriend because he couldn't understand her. She mentioned alienating her family because they couldn't understand her. She'd talked about her friends being fed up. What's Bob Dylan got to do with the price of beer? I'd wondered.

I'd sat back in my chair, placing the tips of my fingers together. "Bob Dylan?" I'd asked.

"That's right," Samantha had said simply. "Bob Dylan."

I'd leaned forward. "Are you saying that Bob Dylan lost you your lover, you mother, and all your friends? What'd he do? Write a song about them?"

Samantha had shaken her pretty head. "No, it wasn't that." She had smiled. "I guess I should start at the beginning . . . you know, with my dream."

"Your dream?" There was no mention of a dream in her letter, either.

Samantha had nodded. "Uh huh. You see, one night about two years ago I had this dream. In this dream, Venus—you know the goddess of love?—Venus came to me and said that I was destined to marry Bob Dylan."

"Venus the goddess of love told you you were destined to marry Bob Dylan?"

"That's right," Samantha had answered. "Her exact words were, "Sammy, forget Archie Bowsmith. He's a nice guy, but he's not the one. Bob Dylan's the one. He's your soulmate, your twin. . . ." She'd looked at me warily, obviously expecting me to react as her friends, family, and Archie Bowsmith had reacted.

I'd nodded in an encouraging manner.

Samantha had continued. "In the morning, I told Archie, my boyfriend? Archie Bowsmith? I told Archie about it and he laughed." She'd made a face. "But you know what men are like. They'll wake you up in the middle of the night because they had a dream about chicken cacciatore, but tell them about something that changed your life and they act like it's a joke."

I'd nodded again, though to tell the truth I was beginning to wonder just how encouraging I really wanted to be.

"Anyway," said Samantha, "I didn't care what Archie thought because I knew the dream was right." She placed a hand on her heart. "I felt it here," she said. "I really did. I knew the minute I woke up that it was kismet, destiny . . . written in the stars: Bob Dylan and Samantha Greenwall, together forever." Her eyes stared off into the distance. Her voice took on a dreamy tone. "I saw us shopping in the supermarket. I pictured us taking the wash to the laundromat. I heard us in the kitchen at night, making decaf. I even knew what we'd name the children. . . ."

"Excuse me," I'd interrupted. "I don't want to stop your story or anything, but are we talking about the Bob Dylan? Bob Dylan, the short, moody songwriter with the weird voice? Not some guy named Bob Dylan who lives in Altoona?"

"The Bob Dylan."

I hadn't been able to stop myself. "Do you know Bob Dylan?" I asked.

Samantha had shaken her head as one might shake off a feather. "Not yet."

"Not yet?" I'd repeated.

"Uh uh." Samantha had smiled then, almost shyly. "But I will."

I'd been rather afraid to ask, but professional training is much stronger than terror. "Excuse me, Samantha," I'd said, "but when do you think this will happen?"

She'd shrugged. "That's the thing, isn't it?" she'd replied. "It could happen anytime."

I'd looked at her a little more closely. Her clothes were immaculate and carefully chosen, her makeup and hair were perfection itself. It must have taken her at least four hours before she was ready to leave the house.

"Anytime?"

"Uh huh. On a bus, on a train, on the street, picking up the cat food."

I'd bitten my bottom lip. "So I guess you always have to be prepared?" I asked at last.

"That too," she'd replied.

"That too?" Even to myself I was sounding like an echo—an echo on the nervous side.

She'd nodded her pretty head. "Well, it's not like you can completely leave these things to chance, is it?" She'd sounded quite reasonable. "You have to make yourself available."

"Available?"

A new energy and enthusiasm had come into her voice. "Yeah, you know. I started hanging out at small music bars because sometimes Bob shows up at places like that."

"Bob?" I'd begun to suspect why she had lost her boyfriend, alienated her family, and given her friends combat fatigue. "Music bars?"

She'd nodded again. "Uh huh. And restaurants. I read all the fan magazines, and I went to any restaurant that Bob ever ate in."

I'd rested my arms on my desk then, my hands folded before me. I'd smiled sympathetically. "Is that why Archie left you?" I'd inquired. "Is that why your family and friends gave up? Because you were hanging out in music bars and overpriced restaurants?"

146

"No." The red hair swung. "It was because of the world tour."

"The world tour? Dylan's world tour?"

She'd shrugged. "Well, his and mine."

Tales of obsessive love are a lot like mallard ducks. If you've seen one mallard duck, you've got a pretty good idea of what they all look like. If you've heard one broken-hearted tale of obsessive love you have a fair concept of how they all go. This one, however, had had some unique details.

"Are you saying that you went with Bob Dylan on his world tour?"

"I don't know, it just seemed so obvious at the time. I figured that if I went to every concert in every city, and sat in the same seat each time, sooner or later he'd notice me. So I gave up my job and I sold my apartment to finance the trip, and I went with Bob on his world tour."

Rarely is a professional relationship-crisis counselor at a loss for words, but it does happen. With some effort, I'd managed to rally. "Are you saying that you followed Bob Dylan around the world? That you went to every night of every concert? That you always sat in the same seat?"

She'd nodded. "I even went to Birmingham."

Once again I hadn't been able to stop myself. "And what happened? Did you meet him?"

A philosophical smile had come to her lips. "I think he must need glasses."

Men: How Well Do You Know Them?

The Quiz

My mother is not only a gifted plumber, baker, and fandango dancer, she is something of a world-class philosopher as well. "Men are like polluted air," my mother is fond of saying. "It may not be good for you, but you still have to breathe it." It was also

147

Althera Beryl Gray who said (as my father, who had been repeatedly warned against trying to repair the roof himself, fell loudly through the ceiling), "It's not that men don't have the sense they were born with. They have the sense they were born with. It's just that they weren't born with that much."

Lest you think that such sentiments indicate any feminist tendencies in my female parent, let me correct that impression right now. As far as my mother is concerned, it isn't men who are the problem, it is women.

"It's like that story about the naked emperor," my mother once explained. "Everyone knew he wasn't wearing anything, but no one bothered to tell him. Instead, they pretended that he was dressed well. They assured him that he looked very handsome in his new suit. They admired the cut and told him that the color set off his eyes."

"Mom," I said. "Mom, what are you saying? That there's a conspiracy among women not to tell men that their flies are open?"

"Try to stay with me, Serena," said my mother. She gave me one of her looks. "The point I'm making is that women know exactly what men are like. They understand them better than they understand themselves. They know precisely what to expect and what not to expect." She made an empty gesture with her hands. "But do they act on that knowledge?" asked my mother.

"Well . . . um . . ." I began.

"No," said my mother. "No, they do not. They sail right on as though they're completely unaware of the way men behave."

"Well . . . um . . .." I stammered. "It isn't always ea-"

"Do they let men know what they really think of them?" my mother demanded. "Do they say, 'Look, Chowderhead, don't start complaining to me that your wife doesn't understand you. She understands you just fine. You're the one who wouldn't understand her if she came with instructions'? No!" boomed my mother. "No, they do not!"

I finally managed to squeeze a word in. "Well, gee, Mom," I said. "You know how touchy men are. What fragile egos they have. . . . I mean, a girl can't—"

Althera Beryl Gray née Siracuso snapped her fingers. "You see!" she shrieked triumphantly. "That's exactly what I mean. Women compensate for men instead of expecting them to behave like adults. Thy make excuses for them. Instead of treating them like the adolescent, egocentric, penis-fixated, insensitive, slow-witted turkeys most of them act like, they carry on as though they think men are normal, rational human beings." She shrugged. "So whose fault is it that these guys never put on any clothes?" asked my mother. "They think they're fully dressed! How could they not when we're always telling them how nice they look?"

Is my mother right? Do women understand men better than they let on? Do we know what men are really like? When we sit together commiserating over a couple of beers and we sob, "Manny, of all people . . . who would ever have dreamed. . . ?" are we really only kidding ourselves?

Here's a little quiz that my mother helped me put together to test your knowledge of the human male.

A. Multiple Choice.

Select the answer that best reflects your opinion and/or feelings.

1. Your boyfriend goes away on vacation by himself for two weeks—a decision that you weren't overly happy about, but in the end you had to respect his wish for independence and space. After all, yours is an adult relationship in which friendship is more important than childish emotional needs. Your boyfriend calls you the day he arrives in Mexico City to let you know that the plane didn't crash. Although you, of course, under no circumstances wanted the plane to land in the Gulf, you wouldn't have been too upset if it had developed a little engine trouble. Just enough to make him

149

sweat. As you say, in all sincerity, "I'm glad you arrived safe-ly, darling," you hear laughter and voices calling your boyfriend's name. "I'd better go," he says. "This is costing a fortune." Aside from one postcard of a pyramid that goes into quite a bit of detail about the cuisine and his bowels, that is the last you hear from him during the two weeks he's away. You throw yourself into your own life and friends for a change. And you have a good time. Such a good time, in fact, that on the night your boyfriend is due to return you are out with friends. It's so late when you get home, and you're so tired, that you go to bed without checking the answering machine. As you collapse beneath your blankets, you are dimly aware of the telephone ringing, but you are far too exhausted to care. You fall into one of those deep sleeps that could only be disturbed by the arrival of the U.S. marines, shooting each other and tripping over the furniture. Sometime on the muddy side of dawn, you are awakened by the sound of at least one marine falling off the ledge outside your bedroom and into the lilacs. It is your boyfriend. When you've finally extricated him, bandaged what could be ban-daged, and given him enough brandy to make him coher-ent, he says that he was hanging outside your bedroom window because when he couldn't reach you by phone he became afraid that something had happened to you. Was he worried that something had happened to you?

   a. Yes, he was terrified. Obviously, he knew that nothing would happen to me while he was thousands of miles away, but that once he was back home anything could go wrong.
   b. Of course he was, he cares about me.
   c. Oh, sure, he was worried. He was worried that I was holed up in my room, playing strip mahjong with Bruce Springsteen.

2. It's your birthday. You drop several hundred hints to your resident male that what you would like this year instead

of the perfume you never have an occasion to use, the electric French fryer/nut cruncher/rice cooker/cherry pitter/etc. that he breaks the first time he tries to use it, or another lace-trimmed slip for your slip collection is a really good set of insulated underwear for a camping trip you and your sister have been planning to Vermont. For your birthday, therefore, your resident male gives you

   a. A slip. He thought you were kidding about the underwear. The good news, of course, is that if he had given you insulated underwear it would have fit the salesman who sold it to him and not you anyway.

   b. Polynesian underwear. You have to admit that it's much more romantic than insulated.

   c. A slip. It's not exactly what you wanted but you appreciate the thought. And it is black and sexy.

3. X (or Scum Breath as he comes to be known amongst your closest friends and acquaintances) leaves you suddenly after ten years of marriage. As it happens, his birthday falls one week to the day after he removes his last tape and Batman comic from your home and into his new bachelor pad. On X's birthday, you grill the rare Miles Davis LP you'd bought him in the microwave and go out on the town with friends. The next day—after a week's total silence—X calls you. Why does he call you?

   a. He just wanted to make sure you're all right. After all, it has been a week since you spoke.

   b. He doesn't come out and say so in so many words but it's pretty obvious that he misses you.

   c. He's upset because you forgot his birthday.

4. The gas bill arrives. Normally your gas bills are around twenty bucks a month, but this one is for two-hundred-and-forty-eight U.S. dollars. Good grief, you think, have we sprung a leak? Has someone opened a Vietnamese restaurant in the attic? You check the bill carefully. It is

marked "Customer reading." You live in an apartment with one other person, and of the two of you, you are the person who always reads the meter because the meter is in the basement and you are the person who isn't terrified of spiders. Except this time. You know you didn't read the meter this time because you were away on business on the date of the reading. When your cohabitor comes home that night you approach him with the gas bill. "Darling," you say. "Darling, who read the gas meter?" Darling

a. says, "No one."

b. shrugs. "It must have been the gasman," says Darling.

c. is so upset over something that happened at work that he doesn't hear your question.

5. Some old friends of yours, passing through town on their way somewhere else, stop by for a visit. Their names are Jack and Janet. Jack, who as it happens is astoundingly handsome for an award-winning photojournalist, is one of your oldest and dearest friends. In fact, it might even be argued that you and Jack are closer than lovers because over the years you have built up the emotional intimacy of female friends without ever jeopardizing your relationship with the jealousy and demands that plague many a romantic liaison. As the evening progresses, and you and Jack start reminiscing and joking and telling the funny-now story of the time you were stranded on an island off North Carolina in a hurricane together, your husband

a. really gets into the party mood and starts drinking as if Budweiser were going out of business tomorrow.

b. starts paying quite a bit of attention to Janet because he can see that you and Jack have a lot to catch up on.

c. begins to sulk because you're paying so much attention to another man and ends up passing out on the floor of the bathroom.

6. By the time you and your life's mate finally turn in for the night, he has given up any pretense of civility. He slams into the bedroom. He throws himself under the covers. You say, "Darling, what's wrong?" He says

    a. "Nothing." This means he's so jealous that as far as he's concerned he might as well have caught you and Jack in the act on the kitchen table.
    b. "Nothing." This means he's in one of his moods.
    c. "Nothing." This means that nothing is wrong.

7. Deciding not to pander to your husband's childishness, you say in a soothing, wifely way, "Don't you think Jack's wonderful, darling?" Your husband

    a. begins to make passionate love to you, to show you how wonderful he thinks you are.
    b. starts shouting the way he does when someone cuts him off on the road. You love it when he's jealous.
    c. behaves like a nuclear bomb that has just had its detonator button pushed. By the time he has stalked off to the living-room sofa, he has not only convinced himself that the reason it took you and Jack so long to make the coffee was because you and he were making something else as well, he has almost convinced you that you and Jack have been secretly seeing each other all through your marriage.

8. Tonight's the night. You and your new love have finally agreed to do the deed. Because you know from past experience that if you didn't remind him about safe sex he wouldn't remember (and because you also know from past experience that if you take the precaution of having a pack of condoms on hand yourself, sometime during a future fight—be it about the exact words to "Stairway to Heaven" or why he's so helpful to the woman across the hall—he will remember those condoms and accuse you of a promiscuous past), the responsibility for buying the

protection has fallen to him. When he arrives, the two of your fall into each other's arms, and you are gratified to discover not only a bulge in his trousers but in his jacket pocket as well. So great is your mutual lust and desire that you are half-undressed before you hit the bedroom, and steaming the windows before you hit the bed. Passion abates a bit when he can't get the pack open. There is another delay while he checks the instructions. And another while he struggles to comply with them. Aware of how sensitive men are, you pretend not to notice and continue showering him with wanton kisses. Yet when you glance at his penis you can't help but say, "Good grief, it looks like a salami!" Does the man of your dreams share the humor of the occasion, or does he

a. collapse like a balloon pricked with a nail.

b. say, "Well, that's that. Now you've ruined the mood," and stomp off to the living room to watch TV.

c. say, "Knockwurst, actually, my little bun," and finishes in two passionate, earth-moving minutes.

9. Your company is expanding, and as a result you've been offered a major promotion. In the short term, it means more money, prestige, and recognition; in the long term it could mean that you virtually write your own ticket. The only drawback to this job—assuming you consider constant sunshine and a house on a beach a drawback— is that it's in California. When you tell your life's partner about this great opportunity he

a. says, "What about your parents?" You, naturally, are touched by his concern.

b. reminds you that there is his career as the manager of a TV repair store to consider too. "You can't just think of yourself, you know," he points out.

c. walks out of the house and doesn't come back until you've gone to bed. He will never say another word about your promotion—not, of course, that he ever said a word to begin with. The day he finds you packing for your move to California, he will again accuse you of never telling him anything.

10. You have decided to visit your oldest and dearest friend in L.A. for a week. Your significant other is

    a. so put out by the idea that you would abandon him like this that he doesn't speak to you for the twelve days before your visit, unless you count, "Where are my orange socks" and "Don't tell me we've run out of milk" as being spoken to.

    b. delighted, of course, that you're going to see your best friend after so long, though he is under so much pressure at work that he doesn't have any time to listen to your plans and won't be able to drive you to the airport.

    c. glad you're getting this much-deserved break, even though, of course, he worries about you in the city. He starts clipping articles on crimes and bombings in L.A. from the paper. He reminds you about how worried your mother gets when you go away and that her heart is weak. "The dog's going to miss you, you know," he says. You find yourself sitting up in bed at night, counting the number of unsolved crimes that happened in L.A. that day.

11. Much to your amazement, your husband didn't forget your anniversary this year. Not only did he send you a card and flowers, he took you out for a romantic champagne dinner as well. As you were sipping your double espresso, he tenderly whispered, "Let's go home, darling. I have a very special surprise for you." When you got home, he presented you with a large silver box tied with a red bow. What can it be? you wondered. Maybe it was that tweed suit you'd been pointing out to him every time you and he passed the dress store. Maybe it was the IBM

software you'd been hinting about. Maybe it was tickets for the vacation in Nepal you'd been longing for. It was a crotchless body stocking. Why did he give you this?

a. Because he thought you'd like it.
b. Because women love to make themselves look sexy for their men.
c. Because he likes it.

12. Your significant other always remembers your birthday. The reason he always remembers your birthday is that:
   a. His mother reminds him.
   b. He cares about you and he remembers. Also, you've written it into his appointment book.
   c. You remind him. It's not his fault he has no memory for dates.

13. You have some friends over after work one evening. You're all sitting in the kitchen, eating pizza and drinking wine and discussing life when your beloved comes home. He doesn't come into the kitchen, but goes straight to the bedroom. This is because:
   a. He doesn't want to disturb you and your friends.
   b. He's had a long hard day and he just wants to collapse in front of the television.
   c. He's pissed off because he thinks you've been talking about him.

14. Same evening, same group of friends sitting around the same table, eating that same pizza and knocking back the same Bulgarian red. Only this time your cohabitor, instead of skirting around the kitchen, comes bursting through the door with a big smile and a "Hi, everybody!" The next thing he will do is
   a. join you. And then proceed to completely dominate the conversation with his interpretation of a movie that no one else has seen.

b. join you. He knows all your friends and enjoys talking to them, of course.

c. join you. He wouldn't want your friends to feel that he was avoiding them

15. It is Valentine's Day. What is your significant other most likely to give you as a token of his affection?

   a. A large red heart filled with chocolates. It's so romantic, isn't it?

   b. A large red heart filled with chocolates. It's the tradition, isn't it?

   c. Chocolates, even though you're on a diet and he knows who will wind up eating them all.

16. Your cohabitor has Friday off. You wish you had Friday off. It's been an incredibly hectic week. The apartment's a mess, the dishes are still in the sink from the dinner party the night before, and you haven't even had time to take the dog to the vet for his infected eye. But you don't have Friday off; in fact it is going to be the busiest day of this frantically busy week. By the time you get home Friday night, you are physically and emotionally exhausted. All during the ride from the office you dreamed of the hot meal and the tidy apartment and the healthy dog who will be waiting for you when you walk through the door. You walk through the door. You have clearly stumbled into an episode of *The Twilight Zone*. Your cohabitor and two of his friends are sitting in front of the television, finishing off a Chinese meal and watching Arnie videos. The dishes are still in the sink from last night, the apartment's still a mess, and the dog still looks as though he's on a crying jag. If you had been home all day, you would have taken care of everything and had dinner and a chilled bottle of wine waiting for your cohabitor. Why hasn't he?

a. It just never occurred to him.

b. He never stops worrying about work.

c. He must have been busy.

17. You and your cohabitor are watching television one night when a new-car advertisement comes on. In it a couple are setting off to visit friends they haven't visited before. The husband is behind the wheel. The wife, equipped with the directions sent them by their friends and a map, tries to act as navigator, but her husband won't listen to her advice. "Of course I know what I'm doing," he keeps saying. "Of course this is the right way." When the couple begin their journey, it is daylight and the car is sparkling clean. By the time they find themselves perched on top of a cliff in the middle of nowhere it is dark and the car looks like it's been on a rather arduous safari in the rainy season. What does your cohabitor think of this advertisement?

a. He's tired of car advertisements and doesn't pay any attention.

b. He can't figure out what it has to do with selling cars.

c. He's annoyed that you find it so funny. He doesn't think that it's funny at all.

18. You and your partner are having problems and agree to separate. Because neither of you wants to separate permanently, however, you agree to seek professional help. The counselor says that the two of you should see as much of each other as you want, but that under no circumstances are you to sleep together. The counselor advises you against physical intimacy because:

a. If you were to sleep with your partner he would assume it was because you were madly in love with him and wanted him back immediately, not because you were feeling feisty or couldn't get out of the habit.

b. Knowing how women are, the counselor is afraid you

might misunderstand your partner's motives for wanting to sleep with you.

c. Women take sex so seriously.

19. He's ill. He caught the flu you had the week before (which more or less went unnoticed by everyone but you), and he's lying in bed, moaning and groaning and checking his lymph nodes, temperature, and pulse every ten minutes—and running you ragged racing up and down with fluids and food and magazines and videos. The reason he is always so much more ill than you are is that:

a. Men are hit harder by illness than women are.

b. Women have to be tougher because they give birth.

c. His mother spoiled him and you've continued the work she began.

20. You've bought expensive tickets for you and your sweetie-pie to see one of your favorite groups perform. As the night of the concert approaches, however, your special someone is in a mood more accurately described as cow pie than sweetie. There are arguments about your family; arguments about his family; arguments about how to defrost the freezer; arguments about Madonna; arguments about how to shift down; a near-brawl in the supermarket over fat-free yogurt. By the day of the concert he has decided that he can't go after all because of pressures at work. You point out that you have been looking forward to this concert for weeks. You mention the small fortune squandered on the tickets. He says, "Why don't you ask Sam to go with you?" Why does he suggest that you ask someone else to go with you?

a. It's a trick. If you go with Sam it will fuel his suspicion—never spoken except jokingly and always denied, of course—that there is/has been more between you and Sam than you've ever admitted.

b. Because he knows that Sam likes this group as much as you and he do.

c. Because he knows how much you like Sam and that you'll have a good time if you go with him.

21. You are in the market for a new computer. Your boyfriend offers to go with you to pick one out. You are, as it happens, something of a computer expert, while your boyfriend couldn't figure out how to turn on an electric typewriter. You tell him that you'd just as soon go on your own because if he comes along the salesman will talk to him and not to you. He
    a. says, "Why don't you want me to come?" Now that you've hurt his feelings he won't come until you promise to buy him lunch.
    b. says you seem a little hypersensitive and glances at the date on his watch.
    c. interprets this to mean that you've been reading Marilyn French again.

22. You set up your new computer and it doesn't work. "Can you believe it?" you rage to your boyfriend. "We drove an hour and a half there and back again and the imbeciles gave me a machine that doesn't work!" Your boyfriend
    a. says, "Um." This means he thinks you've set it up wrong.
    b. warns you not to get so upset. He does worry about your emotionality.
    c. is sympathetic, if a bit distracted by something that happened at work.

23. You go out with your guy and some of his friends from the office. Normally there is at least one other token woman on these expeditions, someone capable of helping you order dinner since the men always insist on going to a Chinese restaurant and then can never make up their minds or end up with six kinds of chicken, but this time you are on your own. Somewhere around the lichees, you rap your spoon on the table and say, loudly and clearly, "Okay, you guys, I've spent several hours listening to you

drone on about work and football and the best route from Jersey City to Buffalo, now we're going to talk about me for a while." Your guy

a. is too busy telling his favorite story about meeting Joe Montana.
b. is too busy dividing the bill nine ways and figuring who had that extra glass of wine to hear you.
c. laughs and says, "Haha, darling, that's very funny," and kicks you under the table.

24. When asked in public why women are so much more emotional than men, your man will give you the look of a dog about to sit up and beg on cue and say, "Because women are more in touch with their feelings." Secretly though, he thinks that the real reason women cry so much is that:

a. Their hormones are responsible.
b. They're mothers.
c. They're more in touch with their feelings.

25. Just for the hell of it, why do you think women cry so much?

a. Because of their hormones.
b. Because they're mothers.
c. Because they live with men.

B. *Yes/No/Don't Know.*

For each of the following statements, indicate whether you agree, disagree, or don't have a clue.

1. If you were telling a story to a group of friends and you got a small detail wrong (the room was blue, not purple) or mispronounced a word (you said Philistayne instead of Philisteen), your life's love wouldn't hesitate to interrupt you with a correction.

2. When you complain to your significant other that he never talks to you, he doesn't know what you're talking about.

3. The three stages in the development of a male-female relationship can be described like so: Phase 1, when you see him as your life's mate. Phase 2, when you see him as your life's work. Phase 3, when you see him as a pain in the butt.

4. Men gossip just as much as, if not more than, women do.

5. Men prefer beauty over brains because men can see better than they can think.

6. There are several men of your acquaintance whom you're careful to avoid being alone with when they've had a drink or two because you know any one of them would make a pass at you. All of these men are either the significant others of your best friends, or best friends of your significant other. You also know that if one of them did make a pass at you, it would somehow be your fault.

7. Men aren't any less devious than women; in fact, one might argue that they're more devious. Let's not forget male behavior like Irangate.

8. Men are less logical and rational than women because men are at the mercy of their penises.

9. After three days of your not speaking to him, he finally asks you, "What's wrong?" "You know," you tell him. "No, I don't," he says. He does know.

10. Men are more possessive than women.

11. Men have an incredible ability to make a big deal out of absolutely nothing.

12. It's true that if men gave birth, there wouldn't be any overpopulation problem.

13. He never listens to a word you say unless it involves his penis or his stomach.

Scoring

In Part A, give yourself a –1 for every B answer. In the odd-numbered questions, give yourself 1 point for every A; 2 points for every C. In the even-numbered questions give yourself 2 points for every A and 1 point for every C.

In part B, give yourself 2 points for every Yes; 0 points for every No; and 1 point for every Don't Know.

If you scored 30 points or lower, you are clueless and living in a beer commercial. Clearly, you have been existing in a male-dominated society for too long and need to go someplace where no one ever sings "I Enjoy Being a Girl."

If you scored 31–62 points, you have occasional glimmers of what makes men tick, but only glimmers. You're still doing a good job of kidding yourself.

If you scored 63–76 points, my mother's right—you do know.

Mother

Many a man, for reasons no one can really explain, wants to marry his mother. Not his real, biological mother—whom he has always found overbearing and singularly unattractive, as well as having no dress sense and an oppressive fondness for ceramic figurines—but a woman who will fulfill all the basic requirements of a mother (usually in a way that his mother did not), plus go to bed with him. "Don't forget to mention that this also gives him someone to blame everything on who is right in the house," says my mother. That, too.

Not that a man will admit to any of this. Asked point-blank whether he is trying to turn you into a young, better-dressed version of the woman who still calls him "Georgie," he will say no.

"Of course I don't want you to be my mother, Valerie," says George. "What gave you a ridiculous idea like that?"

"I think it must have something to do with the fact that whenever I remind you of something you accuse me of nagging."

George smiles. "But, darling, you do nag."

Valerie looks thoughtful. "All I said was that I thought you said you were going to put up those shelves this weekend."

"I said I was going to do it, Valerie," says George. "And I will."

"When?" she wants to know.

Something about the way her thoughtful look has become critical reminds him of someone. He's not sure whom, but he'd rather not pursue it. He leans over and nuzzles her neck. "How could I confuse you with my mother?" he says coaxingly. "My mother smells like Tide and you smell like papaya."

Valerie steps aside. "Don't change the subject."

George flaps his arms in a helpless gesture. "I'm not changing the subject. You were talking about my mother. All I'm saying is you're wrong, I don't think you're anything like my mother."

"Then why do you leave your socks on the floor if you don't think I'm your mother?" she asks.

George gazes at her blankly. "Do I?" he asks.

Valerie folds her arms across her chest, much the way that his mother does. "Yes," she says between clenched teeth. "You do. And you never clear the table. And you leave dirty dishes in the sink."

George shrugs. "Habit," he says. He smiles boyishly. "I lived alone for a long time, remember."

"Toilet seat," says Valerie, squinching up her mouth in much the way his mother did when she found the newt in the bathtub.

"Toilet seat?" asks George.

"Don't tell me you don't know you always leave the toilet seat up," says Valerie.

George doesn't tell her, but his expression speaks volumes.

"Not to mention that you have never once cleaned the bowl."

"Good grief, Valerie," says George. "You sound just like my mother."

Nonverbal Man

I ran into my friend Lonnie in the supermarket one afternoon. I was tapping melons and when I looked over, there was Lonnie squeezing the lemons. We chatted about this and that for a few minutes—she'd had another bout of cystitis, and she wanted to know how my mother's hormone replacement therapy was going, and I showed her what I'd had done to my teeth—and then I said, "So how's Matthew?" Lonnie and Matthew had been married for fifteen years.

Lonnie sighed. "He's all right now, thank God, but I was very worried about him for a while. I thought he might be seriously ill."

"Good grief," I said. "What was wrong?"

We moved over toward root vegetables.

"It was the strangest thing," said Lonnie. "All of a sudden he went off his food. You know what a healthy eater he's always been."

I nodded. "He's the only person I've ever seen order two dinners in a restaurant."

A woman tossing carrots into a bag glanced over. "My brother Larry was like that," she said. "Gave him terrible bowel problems when he got older, though."

165

"He already has chronic indigestion," said Lonnie.

The woman put her carrots in her cart. "Does he fart a lot, too?" she asked.

Lonnie nodded. "Anyway," she continued, "suddenly Matthew just stopped eating. He wouldn't touch his breakfast. He'd skip lunch. He'd pick at his dinner."

"Reminds me of my Terry," said the woman searching through the cabbages. "Same thing exactly. Did he seem a bit listless and depressed, too?"

Lonnie nodded.

"Did you ask him what was wrong?" asked a voice near the cauliflowers.

Lonnie and I both turned. A young woman with a full cart and a toddler had stopped behind us. "Of course," said Lonnie. She started selecting potatoes. "I asked him all the time."

"And what did he say?" asked the woman with the toddler.

"'Nothing.'"

The cabbage woman looked over. "You mean he didn't say anything, or he said that nothing was wrong?"

"He said that nothing was wrong."

"Just like my Terry."

"And then he accused me of nagging him," added Lonnie.

"Just like Larry."

"It just got worse and worse," said Lonnie with a sigh. "I made him all his favorite things and he still wouldn't eat. I begged him to tell me what was wrong, but he wouldn't tell me."

"They're all the same," said the sister of Larry. "Larry's wife was living in South Dakota with a puppeteer and expecting her second child before any of us knew she'd left."

I threw a yam into my basket. "So what did you do?" I asked.

"I made him go to the doctor's with me."

"You'd never get my Terry to the doctor if there was really something wrong with him."

The other women all shook their heads.

"I can't believe he just couldn't tell you what he was anxious about," I said. "Good grief, Lonnie, you've been living with this man longer than most people keep their dogs. Why couldn't he just tell you what was wrong?"

There was a murmur of you-know-what-they're-likes around us.

"So what was it?" prodded the woman with the toddler. "Male menopause? Balding anxiety? Was he afraid he had some terminal disease? My best friend's husband thought he was dying because somebody sneezed on him on the bus and he wouldn't get out of bed for a month."

"It was nothing like that," said Lonnie. She lobbed the bag of potatoes into her cart. She signed. "Turned out he was depressed about going on vacation."

"What?" asked the sister of Larry. "Depressed about going on vacation?"

"My Terry is like that. Hates to go anywhere."

"My husband, too," said the woman whose best friend's husband stayed under the quilt for thirty-one days. "I can't even get him to go to a movie. 'Next week,' he says. 'Maybe tomorrow.'"

"Well, you're a lot luckier than I was," said the wife of Terence. "My Ter was having an affair, that's what was wrong with him. It was guilt."

"It's all either guilt, death, or terror of change," said Larry's sister. "It makes you wonder how we ever got to the moon, doesn't it?"

"Makes me wonder when I'm ever going to see Schenectady," said Lonnie.

O

Old Lovers

Many people often seem to be a lot more fond of the lover they used to have than they are of the one they have now. "Barry never slurped his soup like that," they say. "Ned did everything around the house." Every time you have the snoring argument he says. "Well, it never bothered Zuleika." Every time you wear your batik overalls he says, "Lesley would never have dreamed of going out in something like that."

"It's only natural," says my mother. "After all, old lovers do have certain advantages that current lovers don't have."

Principally that they're not there. They're not there to remind you, and they're not there to remember.

"The problem," my mother says, "is when they are there. Nothing makes a new love more nervous than the presence of an old one."

My mother's thinking about Boris, Marge, and Jim again.

My mother sighs. "So much needless suffering could have been averted if only Boris had gone back to Minsk," says she. "Or at least to San Diego."

Marge and Boris had been madly, passionately, and wildly in love. Only they were incompatible. Put in a confined space

168

together for any length of time—an hour and a half say—they would start squabbling like hungry dogs over a very small bone. They yelled, they screamed, they threw things. Life was never dull, but both of them could see that it wouldn't be very long either if they tried to live it together. Still friends, still soulmates, still close as Warren Beatty's teeth, Boris and Marge broke up.

And then Marge met Jim. He was all the things that Boris was not. Steady, quiet, dependable, caring, giving, even-tempered, and sensitive to others. They fell in love. Jim moved in. Jim met Boris.

"Who is that?" he asked, coming home one night to find a man he had never seen before sprawled across the couch, reading something apparently hysterically funny out loud while Marge fixed dinner.

"It's Boris," said Marge. "Isn't he great?"

"Boris?" Jim repeated.

"I told you about Boris," said Marge. "He's the man I had just gotten over when I met you."

"Oh, right," said Jim, who had heard about the flying kettles and the time Boris threw up all over the table in their favorite restaurant, but not how great Boris was. "I thought he was in Minsk."

"He's back," said Marge.

Back with a vengeance, she might have added. All of a sudden, Jim discovered that he was not part of a couple but one of a troika. Boris was always around. He stopped by for supper. He stopped by for drinks. He went to the movies with them and took them drag racing. He and Marge went mountain climbing while Jim sat in the car because he was afraid of heights. Boris and Marge worked out on the weights together while Jim sat in the car because of his back. Boris and Marge had only to look at each other and say one word—*fork* or *bunny* or *huddle*, for example—to set the two of them off in paroxysms of laughter. Boris knew everything about Marge that there was to know.

"Oh, don't buy her that," he'd tell Jim. "She hates that shade of blue." "Oh, don't give her that," he'd tell Jim. "She read it years ago." "You mean she never told you about Las Vegas?" Boris would say. "You mean she never told you who gave her that tattoo?"

In the end, Jim was so convinced that Boris and Marge were still in love, that next to Boris the Great he was Jim the Joker, that he finally left a note on the refrigerator and moved to Elmyra. Jim, having lost the only woman he ever really cared about, never married, never had children, never knew the joy and love of a happy family. Nor did Marge. Pining for Jim, the nicest man she had ever known and the one man who had ever made her truly happy, she went through a series of meaningless affairs with men like Boris—interesting men who brought out her homicidal tendencies and made her miserable—and eventually opened a souvenir store at the shore.

Years later, Jim and Marge ran into each other on the boardwalk near her store.

"So how's Boris?" asked Jim, speaking the name out loud for the first time in fifteen long years.

"Boris?" asked Marge. "Boris who?"

My mother snuffles back a tear. "That story always makes me cry," she says.

Perfection

Women know that no one is perfect. "No one is perfect," women are always telling me. "We all have our problem areas." Unfortunately, the biggest problem area for most women is men.

A typical woman write: It's not as though I thought Al was some kind of god or something. I didn't. I knew he has this thing about Elvis. I knew he picked his toes in bed. I knew about his temper. I just wanted a human being. You know, someone who spoke the same language I did. Someone I could work things out with. Someone to laugh at my jokes. And what happened? He ran off with a girl who looked just like Priscilla Presley, except she was blond.

Pertinacity

"So how was the barbecue?" I asked Elena when I ran into her at the mall. The last time I'd seen her she'd been buying charcoal and citronella candles.

Elena shuddered. "It was hell," she said simply.

"Hell?" I queried. I must confess that I have never been a big barbecue fan myself. Partly this is because the men always spend so much time arguing about the best way to start the fire and even more time trying to start the fire. By the time the fire is finally roaring, the barbecue chef and his assistants are usually pretty roaring themselves and the women have gone inside to cook the hamburgers in the toaster oven for the children and to have some lemonade and grilled cheese themselves. Nonetheless, *hell* seemed like a strong term.

Elena nodded. "Randy and I had our last fight," she said in a choked whisper.

"At the barbecue?"

She nodded again.

"What happened?" I asked. "Did he drop all the chicken on the lawn or did he fall in the pool?"

"None of the above," said Elena. "It was the apron."

I looked at her in concern. Sometimes the post-breakup trauma syndrome can cause a person to become a little befuddled and confused. "The apron?"

Elena explained. Randy was one of those men who normally couldn't cook a pot of pasta without help, but when summertime rolled around Randy rolled out the grill and went to work with a vengeance. He had a rotisserie. He had the full range of barbecue implements. He had three kinds of barbecue sauce and special plastic squeeze bottles for the ketchup and the mustard. He had citronella candles. He had a chef's hat. He was especially fond of aprons with slogans on the front.

"This year he found one he thought was hilarious," said Elena. She smirked a hollow smirk. "It said: 'I'm Not Opinionated ... Just Always Right.'"

"Oh," I said. It was Randy Ringhorn who once announced to a bemused group of dinner guests that he'd only been wrong once in his life—the time he'd thought he'd made a mistake about something, but hadn't.

172

"Everything would have been fine if it hadn't taken him so long to get the fire going," said Elena.

"What happened?" I asked. "Starvation made the guests a little testy?"

"That, too," said Elena. "But mainly it was because Randy wouldn't take any advice. 'Don't tell me how to light a fire,' he kept saying. 'I was an Eagle Scout.'" She sighed a hollow sigh. "Anyway, finally my mother got really fed up and she went over to the barbecue and demanded to know why Randy would never listen to anybody else."

"And that's what got him mad?"

Elena shook her head sadly. "Not exactly. What happened next was that I pointed to the apron and said, 'I don't know why you're so surprised, Mom. It isn't as if he didn't warn you.'"

"And that's what got him mad."

"Not exactly. He started shouting. 'What's that supposed to mean, Elena? What's that supposed to mean?' So I told him what it was supposed to mean. 'Maybe you should have that slogan tattooed on your forehead,' I said."

"And that's what got him mad."

"Not exactly. But one thing lead to another, and pretty soon we got into the egg argument again."

"And that's what got him mad."

"Not exactly. What really got him was that while we were arguing about how to boil an egg my mother got the fire going."

Q

Questions Men Ask About Women

What is all that junk in their handbags?
What do they do in the toilet all that time?
How are we supposed to know why they're angry?
Why are they always bursting into tears?
What do they want?

Questions Women Ask About Men

Why do they always take up so much room on the bus?
Why don't they ever put the toilet seat down?
Why can't they find the bread knife?
Why are they like that?
Did they ever really believe that we envied them their penises?

R

Relatives

Gina and I were sitting in the car on the freeway, talking about life and the world situation while we waited for traffic to start moving again. I told her what I thought about Eastern Europe.

"So what do you think of someone who would cancel your wedding like that?" asked Gina.

"Have we just started talking about Michael?" I asked. I'd refrained from bringing him up in case the topic was too painful.

"I mean, really," said Gina. "Everything was just great. We were happy, we were in love, we'd chosen the china and put the deposit on the house...."

"It probably wasn't really because of your mother," I told her. "That may be what he said, but it had to be something deeper than that. Something dark and hurtful in his past. Something that tortured him so much that in the end he just couldn't go through with the marriage."

Gina shook her head. "No," she said. "It was my mother."

Gina's mother had come all the way from Seattle for the wedding.

"I tried to warn him about her," Gina continued. "I mean, you know Michael, he's so conservative..."

I nodded. I did know Michael. Michael wore a suit to the dentist.

Gina continued. "But, oh no, he wouldn't listen to me, of course. He knew what mothers are like.

I couldn't suppress a small smile. "If I remember correctly, Michael's mother didn't even raise her voice the time the cat jumped on her back."

"Exactly," said Gina. "It's because they come from New England. Michael's mother's idea of a show of emotion is to kiss you goodbye on the cheek."

"So exactly what happened?" I asked. "Your mother didn't throw the pasta pot at him or anything like that, did she?"

"Oh, no," said Gina. "It was nothing like that. Actually, Mom was on her best behavior. I mean, she did come in shouting because of the cab driver, and there was a little to-do when we went out to dinner and Michael started eating his pizza with a knife and fork, and of course she does tend to be a little bossy with waiters, and I think he was a little surprised when she got up and started dancing with the man at the next table, but he was Italian, too, as it turned out. On the whole, she was pretty toned down."

"And that was it?" I pressed. "You and Michael took your mother out to dinner the night she arrived and the next day he called you up and said he couldn't go through with the wedding?"

Gina nodded. "That was it."

"But that's ridiculous," I said. "It wasn't as if he was going to marry your mother."

Gina started the engine as the car ahead of us moved forward several inches. "But that's just it." She signed. "Michael said that, just around the time my mother was asking him about his past girlfriends and if he'd ever had any sexually transmitted diseases, he looked at her, and then he looked at me, and then he realized that some day I would be her."

"Maybe it's too bad your father didn't come with her," I said. "I mean, if he had met your father he would have realized that you have two parents and that the chances were you were just as much like him as her."

The car lurched forward. "My father couldn't come with her," Gina explained. "My father's in jail."

Revenge

Many people suffering the hurt, pain, and rejection of a broken relationship entertain thoughts of revenge. They shred his best shirts and mail them to him in brown envelopes. They throw all his things on the lawn. They write threatening letters. They try to run down his new girlfriend on their bike. They sit outside his office with a sign that says NEIL RINMAN WORKS FOR THE MOB.

What these people don't realize, of course, is that this is not revenge. It may be madness. It may be masochism. It may be the quickest way to ensure that not only will Neil never have a change of heart, but in years to come, when he's thinking back over his life, there is no chance he will ever gaze up at the moon and think, My only regret is that I didn't stay with Barbara. What he'll think years later as he gazes up at the moon is, Thank God I got rid of that crazy bitch.

No, if you want to avenge yourself on Neil for breaking your heart, the only way is to be happy.

Think of the effect on Neil if, the next time he sees you after your tearful farewell, you are looking better than ever. Beautiful, sexy, vital, filled with energy and life. There he is, trying to get used to living by himself, eating canned spaghetti and lying in his lonely bed at night listening to the bathroom faucet drip. And there you are, doing marvelously without him. Your warm, sensual laughter embraces him. "My God," he says to himself. "She's happy. She's really and truly happy." He glances at the other men passing by, as you sweetly ask him how he is and what he's been doing. The other men aren't looking at him; they are looking at you, their eyes full of admiration and primal lust. A dark, dank thought slips, sluglike, into Neil's brain. Men desire you; they'd probably been counting the days till he got out of the way. A second dark, dank thought follows the first. He believes that he left you because he wanted to kick up his heels a little and have some fun before the last hairs fell out, but now he wonders if you didn't leave him. If somehow you engineered this whole thing. It's obvious that you never needed him. It's obvious that he was holding you back. Four weeks ago he was bored with you. Now he's practically crippled with desire.

If that's not revenge, what is?

S

Self-Delusion

All of Carol's friends had been waiting for weeks to meet the new man in her life.

"Except for me," says my mother.

Except for my mother. Whenever my mother hears that someone has a new man in her life, my mother's heart sinks.

"All those hours of listening to stories about his childhood and his adolescence, and how a sump pump works," says my mother. "I'd rather read a good book."

Finally, a dinner was arranged. As the day approached, we all speculated on what Glen would be like. To date, Carol hadn't been too lucky with men.

"Luck has nothing to do ·with it," says my mother. "If Carol fell in love with a porcupine she d manage to convince herself that it was Jeff Bridges."

"Not this time," Carol assured us. "This time I'm looking at him clearly, rationally, and objectively. This time I'm not fooling myself for a second. I have both feet firmly nailed to the ground and there's no stardust or moonglow in front of my eyes."

"Good grief," say my mother as we met in the kitchen to start

179

serving dinner. "Did she advertise for him or did he just turn up on his own?"

"I think they met in the bank," I said.

"What was he doing?" asked my mother. "Robbing it?"

"I thought you told me never to judge a book by its cover," I reminded her. "Just because he's a little aggressive, and a little . . . um . . ."

"Barbaric," suggested my mother.

". . . rough around the edges . . . doesn't mean that he isn't a very, very nice man."

"He's carrying a gun," said my mother. "Left ankle."

Carol offered to help serve dessert. "Well?" she breathed as the kitchen door shut behind us, "what do you think? Isn't he great? Have I finally found the man of my dreams or what?"

I caught the "or what" on the tip of my tongue. "Well, he does seem very nice, Carol," I said, choosing my words carefully. "And he's very entertaining. . . . That story about the lynching he saw was absolutely fascinating. . . . But you and he don't really seem to have a lot in common."

Carol put the cake plates on the tray. "It's not important," she informed me. "You think that just because I like books and the opera and the theater and he likes cock fighting and greyhound racing and demolition derbies that we're not compatible. But we are."

"Carol," I said, "I bore with you through the Russian sailor. I bore with you through the Greek fisherman. I didn't blink when you decided the love of your life was a man who corrected every second word you said. But, Carol, I can't understand how you and Glen ever met, never mind managed to communicate enough to establish a basis for an exchange of saliva."

"What are you saying, Serena?" asked Carol, instantly defensive. "Are you saying you don't think Glen's right for me?"

"Good grief, Carol, do you have malaria or something? You can't seriously be planning to move in with a man who carries a gun."

"Who spotted it?" asked Carol. "Your mother?"

I nodded.

Carol made a face. "Well, anyway, it's just a small gun," said Carol. "Glen needs it for his job."

"For his job?" I echoed. "And what exactly is his job, Carol? It seems to me he was a little evasive when Althera asked him. Is he a spy? An undercover cop?" I eyed her shrewdly. "Glen doesn't work for the mob, does he?"

Carol laughed. "Of course not," she said, putting the cake on the tray as well. "He's a United Parcel delivery man."

"A delivery man?" I stared at her big blue eyes as they stared back at me, completely sincere.

She nodded. "Didn't I tell you? Don't you think it's wonderful? I've never intimately known a UPS man before.".

"A delivery man?" I repeated. "Where? In Dodge City?"

Carol shook her head. "Oh, no, of course not. In Dutchess County."

"What does he deliver, diamonds?" I inquired. "Since when are the UPS men of Dutchess County armed?"

"Since 1989," she immediately responded.

"Since 1989? Who told you that?"

"Glen told me," said Carol. "There was a rash of robberies of UPS trucks and—"

"Carol," I said. "Can you hear yourself? Do you realize what you're saying? You're saying that you believe that all the United Parcel drivers of Dutchess County have been armed since 1989."

Carol put the teapot on the tray. "Oh, not all of them," She laughed. "Just a select few."

Six Things Men Say That Women Find More Annoying Than a Yeast Infection

1. "Come on, honey, why don't you smile?"
2. "Actually, I'm a bit of a feminist myself."

3. "I hope we can still be friends."
4. "It's not that I don't think you're capable of doing it . . ."
5. "I couldn't help it."
6. "What do you mean I don't talk to you? I'm talking to you now."

Six Things Women Say That Men Find More Aggravating Than Being Stuck in Traffic on the Expressway

1. "You never talk to me."
2. "We never do anything together anymore."
3. "It's in my bag."
4. "You know . . ."
5. "What's wrong?"
6. "We have to talk."

Sport

Men, as we know, are more physical and aggressive than women. Which explains their interest in contact sports. Any game where a bunch of guys run around on a field inflicting serious injury on each other is considered both manly and fun. If, afterward, everyone—participants and spectators alike—can go out and get so drunk they pass out with their faces in their pizza, the occasion is just about perfect. Women don't always appreciate the attraction of this kind of event. They don't naturally like standing in the rain and the cold shouting abuse at the other team. They get confused about the rules. "But why are they kicking the ball from over there now?" they keep asking. "But I thought you said they weren't supposed to use their hands . . ."

Six months into their relationship with Anthony, a distinguished professor of economics at a prestigious university, Cynthia L. came to see me. A mature, intelligent woman, Cynthia was visibly distraught. She and Anthony had met through a personal ad in an academic journal. They both enjoyed Mozart, French food, sailing, Shakespeare, Tolstoy, the theater, opera, and walking in the rain. They had long, open, and revealing conversations as they walked from the theater to the parking lot in the rain. Their minds and souls touched (as Cynthia described it).

"My first husband played football," Cynthia explained. "During the five years of our marriage his nose moved from one side of his face to the other. I hated it when he taped his ears down. He used to push me out of bed in his sleep, dreaming about dropped passes. So I was determined that the next time I was involved with a man it would be an adult, not a beer-swilling twelve-year-old longing for his Cro-Magnon past."

"That seems reasonable," I said.

"You'd think so, wouldn't you?" asked Cynthia. She gulped back a sob. "The first six months were idyllic."

I passed her the tissues.

"And then . . . ?"

And then Cynthia discovered that there was a dark, primitive side to Anthony that she hadn't even suspected—and which he, of course, had failed to hint at, never mind mention.

Cynthia dabbed her eyes. "Last weekend Anthony said he had a big surprise for me. I thought he meant he'd finally gotten tickets to that neo-existential Czech play we'd been wanting to see. But it didn't." She stopped dabbing and swiped. "It meant he was taking me to a football game."

I looked at Cynthia's tweed suit, sensible pumps, and cream silk blouse with the bow at the throat. "Football game?"

She nodded. "The Giants were playing at home." She sniffed. "Anthony's been a Giants fan since he was fifteen. Apparently, he'd rather sit in the rain than walk in it. Football, it seems, is more important to him than Verdi or nouvelle cuisine."

"So what happened?" I asked gently.

Cynthia blew. And then she sniffed some more. "We lost," she said simply.

And therein lay a tale.

Up until Saturday afternoon, Cynthia had been under the impression that she had embarked upon a relationship with a mature and intelligent man who hadn't been twelve for a good thirty-five years.

"Imagine my surprise," she said, "when he started shouting."

"People do tend to shout at football games," I pointed out.

"Not like this," she said. "Even by the standards of a testosterone high, he was shouting louder than anyone else. Several of the other fans told him to shut up."

"And did he?" I inquired politely.

"'I paid for my ticket!' he screamed back. And then he shouted louder." She smiled as a person who just realized that the name of the ship she is on is the *Titanic* might smile. "And then he started jumping up and down and yelling at the players."

"Yelling at the players?"

She nodded. "You know . . . yelling at the players . . . telling them what they were doing wrong."

I indicated that I did, in fact, not know.

"Things like, 'No, no, you idiot, pass it down the middle!' and 'What's wrong with you, are you being paid by the other side?'"

"I guess people do tend to get a little carried away at football games," I pointed out once she'd sat down again. "They usually get a bit more of a response than neo-existential Czech plays."

She eyed me skeptically over her wad of tissues. "It wasn't actually after the game that he got arrested," she said.

"Arrested? By the police?"

"As we were walking—well not exactly walking. I was walking, but Anthony was limping because he twisted his ankle when he fell down the stairs."

"The crowd pushed him?" I ventured.

"No, he was trying to get closer to the field so he could tell

184

the referee what he thought of him and he tripped over his scarf." She took a second box. "Anyway, we were going to the car and we passed a group of Redskin supporters. They were very happy."

"Well, that's understandable."

"Anthony took it personally. He started shouting things about their mothers at them."

"Their mothers?"

"They took that personally. The one wearing the rubber pig snout demanded an apology."

"I'm afraid to ask," I said.

"Anthony said, and I quote, 'The devil will be on ice skates before I apologize to you, you inflatable turkey.'"

"And then what happened?"

"He hit him."

"The inflatable turkey hit Anthony?"

"No, Anthony hit the inflatable turkey. With his briefcase."

"His briefcase?"

"He carries it everywhere. He keeps his cellular phone in it."

"And then what happened?"

"Then the inflatable turkey's friends jumped in and beat the bejeezus out of Anthony."

"I guess the briefcase was a bit of a handicap," I suggested. "In a brawl . . ."

"It was lucky he had it with him," said Cynthia. "I used the phone to call the cops."

T

Take Me Back,
Take Me Back—The Syndrome

Most animals either mate for life or have a take-it-or-leave-it attitude to the whole question of cohabitation.

"If we get along, great," the female animal will say to the male animal.

"Terrific," says the male animal. "That means we'll be able to eat, survive, and raise our young."

The female animal flicks her tail. "But if we don't get along, then that's it," she reminds him. "One of us has to move to another part of the woods. I'm not wasting important time when I could be living wondering where you've been till three in the morning or if you still love me."

"Makes sense to me," says the male. "There's no point drinking at a dry stream."

But humans are different. Humans aren't all that keen on mating for life, but nor are we all that keen on being on our own. We hate change. "Better the dry stream you know than the dry stream you don't know," humans like to say.

And so, clever to the end, we invented a state directly between staying together and separating.

"You mean like an emotional halfway house?" you query.

You could put it like that. It's certainly neither one thing or the other.

"And what is this state called?" you further query.

It's called the Take Me Back Syndrome.

"The Take Me Back Syndrome?" you say. "I don't think I've heard of it."

You have. You just didn't know what it was called.

The TMBS is when a couple who have been living together in incompatible loathing for some time finally decide to call it a day—and then change their minds.

"That's it. Kaput. Finito," they say. Fueled by rage and feelings of injustice and homicide, they go their separate ways, doors slamming behind them. But not for long. He soon discovers that he doesn't like coming home to an empty apartment. She soon discovers that she doesn't like eating by herself in front of the television. He misses having someone to talk to. She bursts into tears when she finds that he's left his favorite Buddy Guy LP behind. He studies all his jackets, looking for one of her hairs (one that, perhaps, he had pulled out during a fight). She leaves the toilet seat up (remembering with something akin to affection the night she fell in). The world is filled with memories of how love used to be: kissing couples, advertisements for romantic weekends, frozen dinners for two. Everywhere she goes, she remembers being there with him. Everything he does, he remembers doing it with her. Pretty soon, one or the other is begging to be taken back. The words "Take me back, take me back" swim in the air. He takes her back or she takes him.

"And that's the end of it then?"

No, that's just another beginning. Because now the world is suddenly filled with memories of how life used to be. In fact, life is how it used to be. The arguments, the misunderstandings, the petty betrayals. They split up again.

"And that's the end of it then?"

Until one of them starts begging to be taken back, it is.

You nibble on your lower lip. "So you'd advise against giving him a second chance?" you say slowly.

Or a third or a fourth. Don't do it, that's my advice. If you're sure in your heart of hearts that it's all over between you and Jeff, then don't let him talk you into trying just one more time. And don't call him up at three in the morning because you thought you heard a burglar at the window.

"Oh, I wouldn't," you say. "Not after last time."

Twenty Things About Women That Drive Men Crazy

1. They're always sitting in the kitchen talking about men.
2. They're so vain.
3. They're so illogical.
4. They're always scheming.
5. The love of gossip.
6. They're so demanding.
7. They blame men for everything.
8. They expect a man to know what it is they're mad about without giving him so much as a clue.
9. The nagging.
10. They're always on the phone.
11. The purse.
12. That they always want to talk about your feelings.
13. The razor
14. Their fixation with your star sign.
15. The crying.
16. That they'll sit next to a perfect stranger on the train and tell that person their whole life story.
17. The moods.
18. The fact that they never fit anything you buy them to wear.
19. That they always hide the corkscrew, your keys, your socks, etc. in a place where you can't possibly find them.
20. The big deal over the toilet seat.

u

Understanding

"Oh, hang on a minute!" cry the men. "We're tired of taking all the blame for everything. Maybe the neutron bomb is our fault. Maybe the hole in the ozone layer is our fault. Maybe you can lay two world wars, Vietnam, Palestine, and the Middle East at our feet, but not everything. Perhaps the trouble isn't that we're so unreasonable. Perhaps the trouble is that women are too demanding. Isn't a guy allowed his passions and flaws? Can a leopard change its spots? Is understanding out of fashion?"

No, of course a leopard can't change its spots. No more than a man can change the fact that he gets a lump in his throat every time he hears "Heartbreak Hotel." And nor is understanding passé. But the trouble isn't that women don't give men a chance. The trouble isn't that women aren't understanding. Women give men a chance. Women do understand.

"I gave him a chance," women are constantly telling me. "I gave him 48,967 chances, if you want the exact figure. And then one day I looked at him and I thought, who is this jerk? If I don't get away from him in the next three minutes I'm going to have to kill him."

"I understood," women are always telling me. "I knew all about his mother. I sympathized about his ex-wife. I never even brought chop suey into the house when he was around because of that experience he had in the take-out by the mall. And then what happened? He gave my cat away. I'd had that cat for fourteen years and I came home one day and it was gone. He was afraid it was going to shred his favorite chair. And I looked at the empty cat's bowl, and I thought about all the unquestioning love and companionship Sylvester had given me, and I thought, who is this turkey? How could I spend hours of my life listening to him rattle on about how his ex-wife never wanted to make love when all the time he was planning to get rid of my cat?

V

Vacations

To a woman a vacation is a chance to get away from work, shopping, cooking and trying to explain to her husband how to work the washing machine. To a man it is a chance to act like he's ten.

—Sophie Tindale, Architect, Wife, and Mother

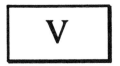

Several years ago, I was sitting in my kitchen, sharing a pot of coffee and thoughts about life with a friend of mine, in the way that women do. Sophie had just come back from her vacation. Had she gone on vacation by herself, she would undoubtedly have returned tanned and rested and whistling a fandango under her breath. But she hadn't. She had gone on vacation with her husband. Because her mother was minding the children for the three weeks, Sophie had wanted to take advantage of this unexpected bonus and go to the Bahamas or Acapulco to one of those resorts where there is nothing to do all day but watch the water level in the pool drop and practice reading in bright sunlight. Bennie, however, wanted to take advantage of the childless vacation to live out a fantasy he'd had since a boy. He wanted to discover Colombia.

"Can you imagine, Serena?" Sophie asked me. "I mean, not only was Colombia discovered several centuries ago, but this is Bennie Hoarfrost we're talking about here. He couldn't discover France if you put him on the plane with a name tag pinned to his jacket and had someone meet him on the other side."

Sophie was right, it was difficult to imagine. Bennie had once spent six hours trying to find Philadelphia, a feat that, presumably, hundreds of people accomplish each day. He still hasn't been there.

So Sophie and Bennie set off to discover Colombia. Bennie made all the arrangements. They landed in Venezuela, their bags went to Brazil, Bennie was allergic to the food, the water, and an indigenous dust mite, and they lost their return flight because Bennie failed to read the fine print on his ticket. He blamed Sophie for this, even though he always insisted on handling the tickets himself, because she has traveled more than he and she should have reminded him. That wasn't the worst part, though, said Sophie. The worst part was the night Bennie decided to tell the patrons of El Flor del Trapiche the story of his life.

I couldn't conceal my surprise. "They spoke English?" In my experience, the residents of small coastal Colombian villages usually stuck to Spanish, if that.

"Oh, no," said Sophie. "They didn't speak English. He told them in Spanish."

"But Bennie doesn't speak Spanish." I reminded her.

Sophie chewed on her teabag. "I know." Sophie said that you had no true concept of humiliation and embarrassment until you had sat in a small, dark bar, packed with people who looked like extras in *Bladerunner*, thousands of miles from home with a chicken on your lap and a man with a one-eyed monkey sitting across from you while Bennie Hoarfrost told, in pantomime and the Spanish he'd gleaned from his guidebook, how he had remodeled his kitchen in Massachusetts all by himself.

"It was the bit where he explained how he'd had to pry the neighbor's cat from the floor adhesive that did it," said Sophie.

"He fell off the table going 'meowmeowmeow' and waving his hands in the air." She spat a few tea leaves onto her saucer and looked at me with haunted, hopeless eyes. "Next time, I'm staying home with the kids," said Sophie, "and his mother can go with him. She's the one who raised him. She deserves to suffer."

Victim of Love

"Where do you think they go for the forty-five minutes there aren't any on the road?" I asked the woman standing next to me on the bus line.

"It's men I don't understand, not buses," she said.

"It's largely men who drive buses," I reminded her.

"You have a point there." She huddled in against the rain and sighed. "Let me ask your honest opinion," she said. "Do you think a man is helpless against his emotions and physical desires, or do you think he has a choice?"

"Pardon me?" I said. "Are we talking about men?"

"It's Ray," she said. "He's having an affair with his secretary. I only found out about it a few weeks ago, when he suddenly got up in the middle of the night and started getting dressed. 'Ray,' I said. 'Ray, where are you going at three in the morning?' And you know what he said?"

"No, but I can't wait to hear."

" 'I'm going to get something to eat,' he said. Those were his very words. 'I'm going to get something to eat.' And he put on his shoes and went downstairs and got in his car and didn't come back for two days."

"Good grief!" I exclaimed. "That's awful. How could he do a thing like that to you?"

"It's not that he doesn't still have feelings for me," she said. "He still has feelings for me. It's me he wants to be with. He's told me that a thousand times. I mean, Melanie's not even very pretty. And she certainly isn't what you'd call smart. And she has one of those very nagging kind of personalities, if you know what I mean. And she can't even type, can you imagine that? She drives Ray crazy, if you want the truth. Absolutely bananas. You should see the state the poor man gets in. I don't think he really likes Melanie very much, if you want the truth, but there's nothing he can do about it. He's helpless against his feelings for her. They just take him over. He has no control."

I tore my mind away from worrying about the possibility that every bus in the city had been hijacked by terrorists. "You mean Ray's powerless against his penis?"

She shook her head. "Oh no," she said. "Not that. I mean, he could take a cold shower if it were only that, couldn't he? Oh, no, it's love he's powerless against. He's a victim. A victim of love."

I stopped looking into the empty distance for something that might be taking passengers. "Let me get this straight," I said. "Ray doesn't really like this woman, he doesn't really want to be with her, he's tried cold showers and aversion therapy, he cares for you and really wants to be with you, but there's nothing he can do about it. The many-clawed and diabolical hand of love has him in its grasp. Even though he's a mature, rational, smart, and experienced man of the world, there is no way he can stop himself from getting out of bed at three in the morning and going to visit Melanie."

"That's it in a nutshell."

Something shimmered in the distance. A charter. "This may sound like a stupid question," I said, "but if Ray really wants to be with you, why isn't he?"

"I told you. Because he's a victim."

I couldn't quite hold back a sigh. "Well, here's another stupid question," I said. "Why do you put up with him?"

She gave me a look of surprise and bafflement. "Why, because I love him, of course."

W

What Do Women Want?

Tom and I were sitting in the kitchen, talking about life and drinking decaf coffee because of his sensitive nerves.

"What is it with you women?" asked Tom. "What is it you want?"

"Oh, you know," I said. "The usual. Global peace. Rain forests. An ozone layer."

He looked at me over his coffee cup. "You're blaming us, aren't you? You're blaming us for perpetual war, deforestation, and the hole over Australia. You blame us for everything."

I put my own cup back in its saucer. "I think that you might be exaggerating slightly," I said.

"I'm not exaggerating," said Tom. "There's nothing that happens on this planet that isn't our fault according to you women. If it rains, it's our fault. If the trains are late, it's our fault. If a relationship collapses after fifteen years, it's our fault."

"Are we talking about Barbara again?" I asked.

"Barbara?" He looked at me in puzzlement. "I don't know why you brought her up. She was the last thing on my mind."

I broke a piece off my French bread. "The thing is that since men do run the world, in a way most of the things that have gone wrong are their fault."

He landed his cup on the table. "So you're blaming me, too," snapped Tom.

"For what?" I asked. "For the destruction of the Amazon?"

"For the breakup of my relationship with Barbara."

I reached for the butter. "Well . . ." I said slowly. "You did have that affair with that waitress. . . ."

He snatched up the butter. "It was meaningless."

I watched as he cleaned out the butter dish. "And the one with the jewelry maker. . . ."

"That was meaningless too."

"And the one with the ballerina. . . ."

He waved his hand. "Nothing," said Tom. "I don't even like classical ballet, and you know it."

"Evelyn."

He scowled. "I suppose Barbara told you that. Don't you women have anything else to talk about besides men?"

What Does She See in Him?

It is a warm and blue-skied day. Erika, Meredith, and Tanya are sitting at a table at an outdoor café, sipping white wine and talking about life, the way that women do.

"Did you hear?" asks Tanya as the conversation about biodiversity comes to an end and Erika tries to catch the eye of the waiter who has momentarily appeared in the doorway. "Marianne's gone back to the dweeb."

The relaxed and contented expressions on the faces of Erika and Meredith dematerialize even faster than the waiter.

"You're kidding," says Erika. "She's gone back to Oscar?" On Erika's lips, the name Oscar sounds about as attractive as the name Hitler.

Meredith groans. "I don't believe it," she says. "I really thought she was through with him this time."

"That's what you said last time," points out Erika.

"That's what Marianne said," says Meredith.

Tanya shrugs. "I don't know if she's taking too many prescription drugs or what," she says, "but she called me last night and she was as happy as a cat in a plastic bag." Tanya imitates Marianne's voice, assuming that Marianne's voice is very similar to that of Olive Oyl's. "Oscar liked the new Mel Gibson movie. Oscar didn't like that restaurant I recommended. Oscar thinks the economy's recovering. Oscar's taking her fishing. Oscar's taking her to a football game. Oscar knows the best place to buy hiking boots. . . ."

"Hiking boots?" Erika hoots. "I didn't know Gucci makes hiking boots," says Erika.

Meredith spits a mouthful of white wine across the table. "Marianne Myrtle's going hiking? Marianne doesn't like to walk to the bus stop!"

Tanya makes the face women make when what is being discussed has no ties with reason or logic—like why the destruction of the rain forests isn't stopped or why Marianne Myrtle has resumed her relationship with Oscar the Dweeb. "Apparently Marianne feels that a lot of her problems with Oscar stem from the fact that they don't share enough of the same interests."

"That's because they have as much in common as a Neanderthal and a starship captain from the planet Muldova," says Meredith, wiping her mouth with a paper napkin.

Erika makes the other face women make when what is being discussed has no ties with reason or logic. "I don't suppose this means that Oscar's going to take up knitting and yoga?" she asks.

"Oh sure," says Meredith. "And develop a passion for Indonesian music and modern dance."

Tanya knocks back her wine. "Apparently Marianne has always nursed a secret longing to go parasailing."

Meredith shakes her head, musingly. "I just don't understand what she sees in him." Meredith turns to her friends. They gaze back.

"Don't look at me," says Erika. "I can't begin to guess."

"Me neither," says Tanya.

"Me neither," says Meredith. "I mean, Marianne's so sophisticated and complex and mature, and Oscar's so . . ."

"I know," says Tanya. "Straight out of the cave with a bone in his nose and a bloody heart in his mouth."

"No wonder she hasn't told him about those years she lived in India," says Erika.

"Not that he ever asked," says Meredith. "If you ask me, he's completely uninterested in Marianne as a person, and she knows it." Meredith rolls her eyes. "Plus he runs around . . ." She lowers her voice. "He even made a pass at me once. Not that I'd tell Marianne that, of course."

"Of course not," says Erika. She rolls her eyes. "Plus he's always borrowing money from her and not paying her back. . . ." She lowers her voice. "He tried to borrow money from me once. Not that I'd tell Marianne. . . ."

Meredith's expression suggests severe nausea. "Plus he's always so rude. . . .

Tanya shakes her head. "And she's always complaining about him. He doesn't consider her feelings . . . he doesn't talk to her . . . he makes a date and then goes off to climb some rock instead. . . ."

Erika stares into her empty glass. "I guess she must be in love with him," she says.

Meredith pushes back her chair and gets to her feet. "I'm going to find the waiter," she says. "I need another drink."

Thought Questions:

1. Why don't Marianne's friends tell her that they feel as safe with her boyfriend as they would with a gaggle of sailors who hadn't touched land for two years?

198

2. Why is it that our lovers so often have nothing in common with our friends? With ourselves? With the Western concept of humanity?

3. What does Erika mean when she says that Marianne must be in love with Oscar? Why does this statement make Meredith rush off for another bottle of wine?

4. If Oscar loves Marianne, why isn't he interested in her?

What Do You See in Him?

Erika and Marianne are sitting in the kitchen, drinking coffee and discussing life as women often do. Marianne finishes what she was saying about Beirut and lifts her cup to her lips. Erika reaches for a cookie. She breaks it in half.

"So," says Erika, breaking that half in half, "I hear you and Oscar have gotten back together."

Marianne nods. "Who told you? Tanya?"

Erika nods. "She says you're taking up parasailing."

Marianne nods. "I've always wanted to get more exercise, you know. The intellectual life isn't really me."

Well, you had me fooled, Erika says to herself. She nods. "And you and Oscar are going to move in together, Tanya says," she says to Marianne.

Marianne nods. "We decided it was time." She carefully sets her cup back in its saucer. "We're not getting any younger, you know."

You mean Oscar's not getting any younger, thinks Erika. He's forty-nine if he's a day. "But Marianne, you're only twenty-eight," says Erika. "That's hardly old."

"It is to start having a family," says Marianne.

A family of what? wonders Erika. She snaps the second half of her cookie in two. "Family?"

"I know what you're going to say," says Marianne before Erika can say anything. "You think I'm making a mistake. Because Oscar and I have broken up so often in the past."

"Well . . ." says Erika, thinking not of the sixteen times in the last five years that Marianne has ended her relationship with Oscar once and for all, but of the fact that Oscar was a married man when Marianne was born, that he is sensitive to the smells of shoe leather and water, that he fights with all her friends, that he doesn't even like the same foods Marianne likes, never mind anything else.

"But it's different this time, it really is," Marianne rushes on. She gives Erika a look of pure reason. "I know Oscar and I have some problems to resolve, but we really want to spend the rest of our lives together."

At least in Oscar's case that shouldn't be too long, thinks Erika.

"Oscar and I really love each other," says Marianne, a note of accusation in her voice that isn't lost on Erika.

"Did I say you didn't?" asks Erika. She picks up the other half of cookie. At least you both love Oscar.

"No," says Marianne. "No, you didn't. But I've always had the feeling that you . . . that you kind of disapproved of Oscar."

Cookie crumbs trickle down Erika's chin. "Me?" she asks, incredulous. "Me?"

Marianne gazes at her cup. "Well, you did say some pretty unkind things about him last time we broke up," says Marianne.

"You caught him with another woman," says Erika defensively. "He owed you five hundred dollars and he wrecked your car."

"Oscar's always felt that you don't like him," says Marianne.

Maybe he's not as dumb as I think, Erika says to herself. "Oscar is a little paranoid. You know that."

Marianne nods. "Oh, I know," she says. "It's because of his mother."

A silence that could be described as pregnant falls, during which Marianne thinks about the damage done to Oscar by his mother and Erika crumbles another cookie.

I can't stand the suspense any longer, Erika thinks to herself as she watches Marianne's pretty face darken with worry over Oscar, his paranoia, and his mother. I have to know. "There is one thing I've always wanted to ask you," Erika says at last. "And I don't want you to think that this is in any way a criticism of Oscar."

Marianne turns to her. "What?"

"Well ..." mumbles Erika. She clears her throat. "It's just that I've always wondered what you see in him, Marianne."

Marianne blinks. "In Oscar?"

No, in Arnold Schwarzenegger, thinks Erika. "Yes," she says. "In Oscar."

"I don't think anyone's ever asked me that before," says Marianne.

I'm not surprised, thinks Erika.

Marianne frowns, in thought and concentration. "Well," she says, "I love Oscar. That's what it is. I love him."

"I know that, Marianne," says Erika. "But why? What is it about Oscar that you love?"

Marianne's frown deepens as she thinks and concentrates even harder. "Well . . ." she says. "He's . . . and . . . well . . ."

Erika decides to help Marianne out. "Is it his looks?" she asks.

Marianne blinks. "Um . . ." she says.

"His character?" prompts Erika.

Marianne chews on her bottom lip. "Well . . ." she says.

"What about his personality?" Erika prods. "Or his sense of humor? Or his great understanding and compassion?"

"Gee," says Marianne.

"Or is it the fact that he likes to climb mountains and crawl though caves?" says Erika. "Is it the model railroad he has in his spare room or that he once shook hands with Nancy Reagan?"

Marianne helps herself to more coffee. "Well, gosh," says Marianne.

"Maybe it's his taste in clothes and furniture," says Erika.

Marianne shakes her head. "No," she says. "No, I don't think it could be that."

"Books?" asks Erika. "Movies? Music?"

"Well, we do both like Chicken Tikka," says Marianne. "And orange juice . . ."

Thought Questions

1. Why doesn't Marianne know what she sees in Oscar?

2. Do you think Oscar would have as much trouble explaining his attraction to Marianne as she has explaining hers to him?

3. Why doesn't Erika tell Marianne what she sees in Oscar?

4. What does Marianne see in Oscar?

Why Can't Women Be More Like Men?

Edward and I were sitting in the living room while I watched him dismantle the remote control and we talked about life.

"I can tell you why things always go wrong between men and women," said Edward.

"You can?"

He nodded. "In a nutshell."

"Well, tell me," I pleaded. "An eager world is waiting to hear."

"It's your fault," said Edward.

"My fault?"

"Women," he explained, flinging a spare screw over his shoulder. "Believe me, I know. After three marriages I'm pretty much an expert on female behavior."

"Oh, do you think so?"

"Yes," said Edward. "I do think so."

"I see," I said. I leaned forward, interested, curious, the good listener my mother had raised me to be. "So what do you think is wrong with the way women behave?"

"They behave like women," said Edward. He stretched out his

legs, making me move out of his way. "If women were more like men there wouldn't be any problem at all."

"You think we should go around starting fights and vomiting at bus stops?" I asked.

He smiled, tolerantly. "There you go like a typical woman, being facetious when I'm being serious." He stuffed something that hadn't come from the remote control into it and closed the case.

"I'm sorry," I said. "I'm not trying to be facetious. It's just that—"

"It's just that women always have to complicate things," put in Edward. He shook his head, looking around on the carpet for something. "Women can never be simple and direct, like a man. If a man doesn't like you, he'll tell you straight out. 'I don't like you,' he'll say. He won't tell you that he likes you a lot but he has to stop seeing you because your star signs are incompatible. If a man's mad at you he won't thump around waiting for you to guess what it is he's mad about, he'll tell you. 'I'm pissed off because you cut me off at the light,' he'll say. And then he'll punch you in the mouth."

"Are we talking about Natalie?" I asked.

"Natalie?" said Edward. "What makes you think we're talking about Natalie?"

"Because you just broke up with her," I said. "Last time I saw you she was the best thing since hair implants and this time you haven't even mentioned her once."

He snapped his fingers. "Natalie," said Edward. "Natalie was no big deal. There are plenty more where she came from."

"Baton Rouge?"

He furrowed his brows. "Serena, please. That's another thing with you women, you take things so literally. All a person has to do is suggest that he might drop by later in the evening and you act like it's written in stone."

"Are we still not talking about Natalie?"

"What is it with your sex? A man says he doesn't want to talk about something and you can't leave him alone." He folded his

203

arms across his chest. He glared at me. "For the last time, Serena, I don't want to talk about Natalie. There's nothing to discuss."

"Okay," I said. "There's nothing to discuss."

"You see!" cried Edward. "That's exactly what I mean." He flapped the remote control in the air, his eyes still scanning the carpet nervously. "You women want to talk about nothing but feelings and emotions. You feel left out. You feel cut off. You feel used and taken for granted. Never mind logic. Never mind a good, stimulating intellectual discussion."

I struggled to keep up with the march of logic. "You mean a stimulating intellectual discussion about why women don't behave as men behave?"

"Yes," said Edward. He was beginning to raise his voice. "That's exactly what I mean." He pointed the remote at himself. Something fell out. "I'll tell you one thing," he said. "If I were Natalie I wouldn't have gone off like that. I would have understood."

I thought I could see a little flaw in the logic here. "Not if you were a woman you wouldn't," I pointed out.

Edward looked at me, grumpily, suspiciously. "You see what I mean?" he shouted. "Women can never stick to the matter at hand."

I reached over and picked up the screw he'd tossed away and handed it to him.

"What's this?" asked Edward.

"It's the screw you were looking for," I said. "So you can close the remote."

"I wasn't looking for it, Serena," snapped Edward. "I knew exactly where it was."

Why Women Cry

Yet another thing about women that puzzles many men is why they have such a propensity to tears.

"You see them weeping all over the place," one of my clients,

Mr. G, once commented. "On buses, in movies, on street corners, in the kitchen ..." He shook his head, sadly. "All you have to do is say one little thing about the soup or their hips and away they go. Sometimes you don't even have to say anything," he want on. "Sometimes all you have to do is look over from the news and she'll burst into tears."

I asked him why he thought women cried so much. "Do you think it's because they're more sensitive and in touch with their feelings than guys are?" I ventured. "More emotionally honest and open?"

He shrugged, baffled. "I think it must have something to do with their ovaries," he said.

My friend Amanda has a different theory.

"The reason women cry so much is because of men," says Amanda.

Because they're always breaking our hearts?

Amanda shakes her head. "No, because they drive us nuts."

What happens when you're ill? When you're ill, you stagger along, doing the chores, making sure there's milk and cat food in the house, not allowing a fever and sore throat to let you forget your mother-in-law's birthday or to wash little Benjy's shorts in time for gym.

What happens when he's ill? When he's ill he takes to his bed for five days, feeling his lymph nodes every half hour and making everyone crazy with his demands and complaints.

What happens when you have to sit next to a man on a bus? He sits there with his legs spread open, taking up two-thirds of the seat, and you spend the entire journey clutching the seat in front and trying to keep from landing in the aisle.

What happens when he wants you to watch the Norwegian movie with him that's on the television and you don't. You say, "Actually, I think I'll just putter around and maybe write some letters, Nick," "What?" says Nick. "But I thought you wanted to watch the movie with me." "No, you wanted me to watch the movie with you. I find those Norwegian movies too depressing.

I'd rather take a bath." "But you should see it," says Nick. "It's a very important movie." "Not to me it isn't," you say. "You're going to make me watch it all by myself?" says Nick. In the end, the argument becomes so heated that Nick storms off to the bedroom to sulk, and you wind up in the living room, watching a movie about a long and—from what you can gather—depressing weekend in the woods in a language you can't understand.

What happens when you want to have sex and he doesn't? Nothing.

What happens when he wants to have sex and you don't? First he's sweet and affectionate and coaxing. Then he starts sulking. Then he stomps out to the couch taking all the covers with him.

Amanda says that, when you get right down to it, men are basically self-centered and self-involved. Everything that happens to a man is a big deal. If he gets a cold it's pneumonia. If the store's run out of his favorite cheese it's a world famine. If he had a nice time gutting fish with his dad when he was twelve it's a mystical experience. If someone puts a dent in his car or shrinks his silk shirt he's traumatized for weeks.

Men spend so much time worrying about themselves that they barely notice there's anyone else on the planet with them.

"Get real," says Amanda. "Unless a man wants something—a sandwich, or a back rub, or an exchange of bodily fluids—he acts like you're not really there."

So what you're saying is that women aren't prone to tears because of their hormones or their delicate natures.

"That's right," says Amanda. "They weep buckets because it's the only way they can get any attention."

Xenophobia

Mary L. threw herself into the chair with a gasp of exasperation. "I can't believe it," she said. "I just can't believe this is happening to me."

"What is it?" I asked, gently and compassionately. "You love too much? You're addicted to romance? You have a tangled history of failed and misguided relationships?"

"Worse than that," she said. She ran her fingers through her hair. "Here I am, a right-thinking, liberal kind of person. I don't eat meat. I don't use aerosols. Every soap, cleaner, and paper product I use is environmentally friendly. . . . And what happens?"

I leaned forward. "What happens?" I pressed her.

"I'm becoming a xenophobe, that's what happens," Mary L. wailed.

"A xenophobe? You're afraid of foreigners?"

She nodded vehemently. "Terrified."

"How does this terror manifest itself?" I inquired.

"I screen all telephone calls. I dress in dark, drab colors so as not to call attention to myself. You know what happens when you call attention to yourself, they start talking to you and asking pesonal questions. Even wearing my black coat and my black scarf, I never allow myself to get into a situation where I might be alone with one for any length of time. Even if you pretend to be busy reading something or studying the ceiling cracks, they're bound to start babbling on about the invention of plastic wrap or politics in Guatemala. It's gotten so bad that if one of them stops me on the street to ask for directions I keep right on walking. I mean, I know it's rude, but so many times you think all they want to know is how to get to the bus station when what they really want is to tell you what they think of your bra size."

Paranoid delusions, I wrote in my notes. I looked up. "I can see this is beginning to get out of hand," I said.

She flapped her arms. "You're telling me? You know what happened yesterday?"

I shook my head.

"Yesterday I was in the supermarket and one of them came up to me wanting to know where the crispbread was, and I wouldn't tell him. Can you believe it? I knew the crispbread was between the jams and the gourmet olives—I mean it took me two months to find it because it's just where you wouldn't expect to find it. But I wouldn't let on. I couldn't shake off the thought that if I said, 'Aisle six, sort of near the bread crumbs,' the next thing I knew I'd be embroiled in a half-hour discussion of why I didn't smile more."

"You're really going to have to go into intensive therapy," I told her solemnly "Are there any particular foreigners you feel like this about, or is it a general terror?"

Mary raised her eyes to mine. "Oh, it's specific," she assured me. "It's only men."

"Men? You mean it's not Canadians or reindeer herders, it's men?" I started crossing out *paranoid delusions*. "Why didn't you say that in the first place?"

Y

Yutzing Around

Yutzing around is a term often used by Althera Beryl Gray.

"It's from the transive verb *yutz*," she explains. "Anglo-German in origin, *yutzing* means using wish-washiness and indecision to avoid saying or doing what you really intend to do or say, usually for the purpose of hedging your bets."

We're not still talking about men, are we?

"No," says my mother. "We're talking about your Aunt Edith."

My Aunt Edith is, by anybody's standards, a champion yutzer. She hates hurting people's feelings.

"Feelings, schmeelings," says my mother, who is not afraid of hurting anybody's anything. "The reason your Aunt Edith wound up in Thailand with that exiled Chilean painter during the rainy season wasn't because she's too sensitive. It's because she always wants everyone to like her. It's a common problem." She clicks her teeth. "Though not one we share."

My Aunt Edith, already married to Rudolph, the Russian flautist, met the Chilean painter, Miguel, in New Paltz the summer Rudy was in Flagstaff. Miguel fell madly in love with Edith at first sight. Edith was actually physically repulsed by him, not being overly fond of short, dark men, but of course she didn't like to tell him that she didn't find him even minutely attractive—if she told him he might not be interested in her anymore—so she agreed to go out with him one evening.

"Yutz number one," says my mother.

The evening went well. Miguel turned up with an armload of flowers and a bottle of champagne and a sketch he'd made of her from memory entitled *Edith on the Upstate Bus Before It Crosses the River*. It did occur to Edith at that point that a discreet mention of Rudy and his flute might give a slightly better perspective to things as far as Miguel was concerned, but he was so sweet and so attentive and she didn't want to sprinkle the rain of bad news on his emotional good day. So she didn't mention Rudy. And when Miguel went to kiss her good night she didn't have the heart to move quickly so his lips hit the wall behind her.

"Yutzes two and three," says my mother. "You can see she was building up speed."

By the end of the week my Aunt Edith had built up so much speed a police blockade wouldn't have slowed her down. Miguel had more or less moved in and was teaching her how to speak Spanish. Rudy's things were packed away in the attic, so as not to cause Miguel to ask any difficult questions concerning men's suits and hiking boots about the right size for Bigfoot.

"Yutz, yutz, yutz," says my mother.

Miguel started talking about marriage. Edith didn't exactly say yes, of course—well, she couldn't, could she, since she was already married—but she didn't say no, either. Instead, she said she was going to Thailand. Thailand, she felt, was an inspired choice because Miguel wouldn't be able to follow her there. That is, he could follow her, but he wouldn't be allowed back into America if he did. Ergo, he wouldn't follow her. When he did follow her, instead of saying, "Miguel, *amor mio*, there's something I have to tell you," Edith said, "What a surprise?" "Are you glad to see me?" Miguel whispered. It was Edith's opportunity to whisper back, "Not exactly." But she didn't want to hurt his feelings.

At this point in the story you might very well be wondering what had happened to Rudy. He'd picked up a bit of color in Flagstaff, he'd acquired a taste for Mexican food, and he was looking forward to getting back to New Paltz and seeing his wife. Only, of course, his wife wasn't in New Palz, she was in Thailand, a fact she had neglected to mention to Rudy in case it upset him at a crucial stage in his career.

"How many yutzes does that make?" asks my mother.

Edith later admitted that she could see, in retrospect, that there were several junctions in this saga where a simple yes or no would have set everything straight. At the time, however, she couldn't quite see it like that. If she said yes to Miguel she would have to give up Rudolph. In either case, someone would be hurt.

"Or mad at her," amends my mother.

Meanwhile, Rudy was about to go back to New Paltz but Edith was stuck in Thailand with Miguel because Miguel couldn't go back to New Paltz or to Chile and she couldn't bear the thought of telling him she was returning without him. She wrote to Rudy telling him how much she missed him and was looking forward to seeing him but that the rains had washed her passport away so she was going to be delayed.

Rudy turned up in Thailand, too.

"It was starting to get pretty crowded in that bamboo hut," says my mother.

Rudy and Miguel were surprised and, one assumes, less than delighted to make each other's acquaintance. When things settled down, each man turned to my Aunt Edith and said, "Well, Edith, which of us is it to be?"

My aunt excused herself for a few minutes, sneaked out the back, and took the first plane to Detroit, the one place, she reasoned (rightly), no one would think of looking for her.

"Once a yutz, always a yutz," says my mother.

Z

Nothing begins with Z. That is, quite a few things being with the letter Z—*zoom* and *zest* and *zygote* and *zeal*—but nothing that really fits into the relationship game unless you count *zilch* (as in? I gave him everything and he gave me zilch).

So my mother and I have decided to make Z stand for

Zone

I can hear you chortle. You think we mean zone as in "battle zone." "Well, that makes sense," you're saying to yourself. "Most couples do more combat duty in a year than your average commando will experience in a decade."

Oddly enough, though, you're wrong. We mean zone as in "an area with particular characteristics, purpose, or use."

For the real function of a relationship is not to divide and separate and drive you to drink, but to create a place (a zone, if you will) where two people from different backgrounds—or, in the case of men and women, planets—can spend their time, energy, and emotions trying to step beyond the things that divide them to get to know one another in a real and meaningful way.

"It isn't easy," says my mother. "It's a difficult and often thankless task. A lot of the time we're doomed to failure. Most of the

212

time you'd probably spend your time better if you were to try digging a swimming pool with a teaspoon." She sighs. "Some-times, I suppose, you might even wonder why anyone bothers."

Well, yes, you say, that thought has occurred to me.

My mother shrugs. "What else have we got?" she'd like to know.

About the Author

Serena Gray is the author of *The Slag's Almanac*, *Beached on the Shores of Love*, *Life's a Bitch . . . and Then You Diet* and *The Alien's Survival Manual*. She splits her time between New York City and London.